T0370396

Revealing a Heavenly Father to a fatherless generation!

- Jesus Christ is the exact representation of the Father!
- Heaven's Operational System: Families: Father and sons!
- Heaven (Kingdom of God) looks like Family!
- The Spirit of Father raises spiritual fathers who will raise and empower the sons of God!
- We do what Jesus did ... revealing the Father!
- How to father God's sons and daughters
- Developing leaders into spiritual fathers who will be able to raise the sons of God

FATHERHOOD
UNIVERSITY

DR. SAREL VAN DER MERWE

WESTBOW
PRESS®
A DIVISION OF THOMAS NELSON
& ZONDERVAN

WestBow Press books may be ordered through booksellers or by contacting:

WestBow Press
A Division of Thomas Nelson & Zondervan
1663 Liberty Drive
Bloomington, IN 47403
www.westbowpress.com
844-714-3454

Because of the dynamic nature of the Internet, any web addresses or links contained in this book may have changed since publication and may no longer be valid. The views expressed in this work are solely those of the author and do not necessarily reflect the views of the publisher, and the publisher hereby disclaims any responsibility for them.

Any people depicted in stock imagery provided by Getty Images are models, and such images are being used for illustrative purposes only. Certain stock imagery © Getty Images.

All scripture quotations are taken from the New King James Version®. Copyright © 1982 by Thomas Nelson. Used by permission. All rights reserved.

ISBN: 979-8-3850-0679-3 (sc)
ISBN: 979-8-3850-0680-9 (hc)
ISBN: 979-8-3850-0681-6 (e)

Library of Congress Control Number: 2023917251

Print information available on the last page.

WestBow Press rev. date: 3/7/2024

DEDICATION AND THANKSGIVING

I want to dedicate this book to my family; my wife Thiesa, my sons and their beautiful wives and my nine grandchildren, who are such a blessing in my life. Thank you for your sacrifice, passion and love and for supporting me on this journey.

Also, thank you to my spiritual sons and daughters and many students who have been the testing ground for countless ministry experiences.

A special thank you to the many friends who contributed to this book's writing and editing.

Thank you, Jesus, my Saviour, who introduced me to my ABBA Father and baptised me into His Holy Spirit. Thank you for your presence and guidance in my life journey and for preparing and equipping me for each new season.

Spiritual fathers (and mothers) who inspired me to Fatherhood:

Bethel (Redding, U.S.A.) team: Bill Johnson, The Johnson family, Kris Vallotton, Paul Manwaring, Steve Backland

Heidi Baker, Derek Crumpton, Charlotte Cronk, David Wagner

Books that influenced me to become a better father:

You have not many fathers: Dr Mark Hanby

Healing the orphan spirit: Leif Hetland

Father and sons: Angus Buchan

The spiritual mentor: Ron Depriest

Where are the sons in the House: Jerome Nel

I need a father: Guillermo Maldonado

The cry for spiritual fathers and mothers: Larry Kreider

Experiencing Father's Embrace: Jack Frost

God Distorted: John Bishop

The father connection: Josh McDowell

The Father Heart of God: Floyd McClung

The Fatherhood Principle: Dr Myles Munroe

My Father! My Father! Sam Soleyn

On Daddy's shoulders: Tommy Tenney

The search for lost fathering: James Schaller

Fathers in the House: Bishop Tudor Bismark

The order of a son: Dr Mark Hanby

Fatherhood of God: JS Lidgett

Fathered by God: John Eldredge

CONTENTS

CONTENTS

FOREWORD

David Wagner, an international prophet

I am convinced that 'Fatherhood University', written by my dear friend Sarel van der Merwe, is one of our day's most important, needed, and timely books. I remember meeting Sarel for the first time at his home in South Africa in 2011. As I shook his hand and looked into his eyes, I could tell there was something remarkably different about this man of God. When he looked at me, it was as if he was looking at me through the eyes of The Father, and when he spoke, I could hear and feel the Father's heart in every word. As I spent time with Pastor Sarel, I took note of the strong apostolic and leadership gifts in his life, but what impressed me the most was the fruit that I saw in his life that was evident in his marriage to his wonderful wife Thiesa and his relationship to his amazing sons, daughters-in-law, and beautiful grandchildren. Over the years, I have watched what Sarel teaches and preaches line up with how he leads his ministry and lives his daily life. I am thankful that I have been blessed to be given a friend who constantly and consistently reveals "Abba Father" to all of us. Undoubtedly, we are living in unusual days where the world and even the Church have lost its identity, moral compass, truth, and way. However, there is a solution to the crisis, and I believe that that solution is found in true spiritual Fathers who know how to demonstrate how to love, lead, guide, and reveal The

Father to us. In 'Fatherhood University', Pastor Sarel shows us how Jesus truly and precisely represents the Father to us and teaches us God's desire and design to manifest Heaven on Earth through Kingdom Family. I often say, "You don't need to be prophetic to know the problem because problems are everywhere, but you do need to be prophetic to know the solution." In writing 'Fatherhood University, ' I believe that Sarel van der Merwe has faithfully stood in the council of The Lord to hear The Father's voice and heart to bring the healing solution to a fatherless generation. 'Fatherhood University' is brilliantly written to equip, empower, and encourage people to discover the heart of God the Father. This book is deeply spiritual and yet uniquely practical. As I read through the pages of this book, I found areas of my heart being healed and awakened as I was led into a deeper understanding and revelation of The Father and His great love for me. I trust that 'Fatherhood University' will change your life just as it has changed mine. I am thankful for this amazing book and the transformation it will bring to the world and the Church.

David Wagner
Father's Heart Ministries
Franklin, Tennessee USA

Pastors and leaders must learn how to 'father' their own people in their Churches. They must also be healed from their father wounds to become great spiritual fathers.

Pastors, leaders, and Christians should also be "fathered" by healthy, real apostolic fathers!

INTRODUCTION

This book may be one of the most needed and in-season books for the life of the Church and for the endangered disappearing species called 'healthy godly families'! Don't only read the first chapters because fresh and much-needed revelation will keep jumping out of the pages as you keep reading! This book is also for daughters of God who want to operate in the Spirit of the Father!

God clearly called me, and notable prophetic people confirmed that God called me into fathering His people. At first, when I heard this twenty years ago, I thought it was what I was already doing as a pastor. Ten years later, I realised that I didn't know what I was supposed to do as a spiritual father. Another ten years later, I feel that I now understand far more and sense the anointing of Father God to father His people. David Wagner (renowned international prophet) prophesied that God is not only raising me to father many sons and daughters but that I would also write a book called 'Fatherhood University'! So here I am, obeying the voice of God and trusting Him to shake the Church and nations with this word in season.

I am privileged to be actively involved in the lives of dearly beloved sons and daughters who have committed themselves to my wife and me to be mentored and fathered. Our ultimate goal is to help and support them to maturity and then to release and send them on their journey to fulfil their Godly calling. We will be there for them as long as we live and are able to cheer them on to reach their goals.

Wherever a significant truth surfaces within the body of Christ, a counterfeit of the original will always develop. When God started to speak to the Church again concerning prophets, it seemed everyone turned into a prophet. Recently, much has been said concerning the restoration of apostles in the Church. Many pastors and prophets changed their titles to apostles. However, Apostle is not a title; it is a function of an anointing given by God to a few.

With the resurgence of the order of father and son in the ministry, many will announce themselves as fathers and sons. They will seek honour not due to them and submission that is not their right. They will not be true fathers or sons in the ministry but fake imitators.

In the time of the judges, the Bible tells us, **"In those days there was no king in Israel; everyone did what was right in his own eyes." Judges 17:6 (NKJV)**

The fulfilment of God's ministry pattern is often perverted by turning men's hearts toward financial gain instead of fatherhood.

Fatherhood is born through true sonship! Sons flourish in the presence of real fathers!

Becoming a good father is not automatic; it takes time and effort. Fathering is a full-time job, and we must be willing to invest in this job. It is more important, second to being a husband than any other career we pursue. A father should present the fundamental qualities of leadership, responsibility, accountability, and the capabilities of planning, discipling and loving. As men, we must train, develop, and learn to be what God intended for our families.

Fathering is more than just a natural function, which extends beyond gender if it is what God has put in you to be and accomplish. Effective and impactful fathering is not easily explained because it imparts the intangibles.

You may ask; What about spiritual mothering? As the Church has been described as the mother and God as one who mothers her children, we must recognise that mothering is also very important. It is like a family, whereby the family needs a dedicated mother but realises that most of the children's identity comes from the presence of a father. Maybe the topic of mothering may be another book in the future! Currently, most Churches practice mothering through their pastors more than fathering.

If you are a pastor or a leader in the Church of Jesus Christ, then I hope and trust that you will have a significant ABBA Father encounter through the message of this book! Becoming a great father to your Church family is a unique and honoured task that is impossible without God's calling and Father's anointing! I pray that the Spirit of the Father will fill you and that your understanding of God's purpose for the human race will become more evident.

Creation is in frustration waiting for the manifestation of the sons of God, according to Paul, the Apostle.

For I consider that the sufferings of this present time are not worthy *to be compared* with the glory which shall be revealed in us. For the earnest expectation of the

creation eagerly waits for the revealing of the sons of God. For the creation was subjected to futility, not willingly, but because of Him who subjected *it* in hope; because the creation itself also will be delivered from the bondage of corruption into the glorious liberty of the children of God. For we know that the whole creation groans and labours with birth pangs together until now. Romans 8:18–22 (NKJV)

Let the sons of God rise and take dominion of the earth!

What could your ultimate blessing in discipleship and spiritual growth be?

Suppose you can have a healthy, mature, earthly spiritual father who cheers you on to fulfil your divine calling! It would be like Father God Himself taking your hand and leading and encouraging you to become what He made you to be!

MY JOURNEY OF UNDERSTANDING FATHERHOOD

My experiences and memories of my father might be much better than most other men. And though I have some unique and fond memories of my father, I also have painful memories of his behaviour and relationship with me. He taught me many life skills and supported some of my sports and hobbies. However, some severe gaps in my understanding of intimate and unconditional love were left open. Even though I failed in both, I tried to impress my father with many things, like sports and academic results, to get more acceptance as a son. I always felt less important than my siblings. Compared to my peers' families, my father and mother raised me in a very 'normal' way. My father lost his father at an early age and did not know most of the dynamics of fathering. His work took him away from home for many months and left a significant father-figure absence in the home. My mother did her best to raise her three children according to her knowledge of child education and formation.

The most significant pain and separation came years later with my father's inability to accept and understand my passion for Jesus. My priority and focus for Jesus' Kingdom and Church caused the greatest separation in our relationship until his death.

As a young teenager, I was looking for the embrace and relationship of my father. I connected with the wrong crowd as a kind of substitute for a male mentor who had a very negative input on my life. By smoking and participating in some minor criminal behaviour, I got in deep trouble with my parents and school. As a young man trying to find my identity, I got confused with false religious behaviour and wrong sexual interest. My life changed dramatically after my conversion to Jesus at the age of nineteen. But still, there was a great void in mentorship and spiritual fatherhood.

Painful memories of a partially absent father, abusive older brother, failing Church leaders, and destructive schoolteachers took years to heal and restore.

Becoming a father to my own three boys continuously challenged me to evaluate my understanding of fatherhood. Reading books and observing healthy families taught me many principles of Godly child-raising and fatherhood.

Many unique mentors, spiritual mothers, and fathers who greatly influenced my understanding and showed me correct behaviour came into my life. God took me through many memorable encounters in which I personally discovered and experienced God the Father. Knowing who God is may make you a good teacher, but to experience Him personally as your Father (ABBA) requires a unique relationship and intimate encounter, which very few people have experienced.

The more I understood what God expected from His Church to father a fatherless world, the more I sought a spiritual father who would be more than just a good mentor in my life. Many leaders who lead through control and spiritual manipulation came into my life and taught me how ABBA Father does not operate! Connecting to leaders who did not serve with a heart

(Spirit) of the Father caused even more discouragement and withdrawal. I sometimes felt like Moses, fathered by Egyptians (ladies) for forty years and then another forty years by a father-in-law and God (his Friend) in the desert. He had to lead and father more than a million Hebrews through the desert and become a great influential father to Joshua, Caleb, and their descendants. They, eventually, would enter the promised land. God can turn any dysfunctional past into a building block for a strong future.

One of the most significant discoveries about my understanding and revelation of the Father is this, the process of healing and renewal of my mind is a lifelong journey which is needed to comprehend the nature of ABBA Father more and more increasingly. So, the journey and growing in deeper intimacy never stops. There is always more!

After God spoke to me to father His people, it took me many years to comprehend the meaning and depth of the calling. Revealing the Father to a fatherless generation became my life motto and my personal desire to be the Truth that Jesus came to reveal ... the Father!

I'm so thankful for my three sons, who were my testing ground, on which I made mistakes, learnt through trial and error, and finally, how to apply Godly fathering. Any wounds I may have caused as a father have been restored through them going through their own healing process. They have become powerful, influential fathers, husbands, and leaders in the Kingdom of God.

You cannot teach others something you do not live and experience (you can't give what you don't have)! Apostle Paul as a spiritual father, said, 'Imitate me!' In this writing, I want to share some of the powerful revelations I have received from

ABBA Father, and maybe I can say with Paul: Imitate me as I am imitating Jesus Christ and ABBA Father. This book is just another giant step towards knowing Him more and having a more excellent intimate relationship with Father.

It takes a mature father to write about fatherhood and a real son who intimately knows God as Father to reveal His heart to His people and the fatherless generations! This lifestyle is what I have chosen to be and to do!

"...having His Father's name written on their foreheads." Revelations 14:1 (NKJV)

Where have all the Fathers Gone? Gone?

We are living in the most fatherless generation in history, where men are not absent because of war but have chosen to flee from the family ship.

So, what's the problem? Why all the fatherlessness?
In the 1960s, the foundation for fatherlessness was laid. The Sexual Revolution's message was loud and clear: free love meant making love to anyone you're with, but no commitments, no covenants.

Now, let me be clear: immorality has existed since the beginning of time. But, it was normalized in the 1960s.

The sexual revolution created the perfect environment for Darwinism to emerge. People were violating their own moral values and were looking for a way to avoid answering to God for the guilt they were experiencing.

Charles Darwin gave the world the excuse it needed to live like hell and not answer to heaven. Whether you agree with Darwin or not isn't as important as understanding that his "scientific" theories have led us to cultural mindsets that have ultimately been destructive to human dignity and morality.

Such a philosophy naturally elevates pleasure as the highest goal of life on this "godforsaken" planet.

The Societal Effects Are Shocking! Here is a brief overview:

Children living with a mother only is the second most common U.S. living arrangement, a number that has doubled since 1968.

In 1950, less than 5 per cent of all children were born out of wedlock in America. By 2017, that number rose by more than 1,700 per cent!

The outlook may seem bleak, but there is hope!
The drought of fatherhood has crested on the mountain of selfishness and isolation. That mountain is about to be washed away by a deluge of conviction and compassion — a mighty outpouring of God's Spirit.

(Used with permission from Kris Vallotton from Bethel Church, Redding. California, USA.)

1. A FATHERLESS GENERATION

Think about God right now. What comes into your mind? What feelings or images come to you? What does He "look" like to you? How do you think He feels about you? Be honest; don't give some churchy answer you think you're supposed to give if that's not what you really feel deep inside.

So, what is the first thing that comes to mind when you think of your earthly father? Provider? Teacher? Generous? Funny? Or perhaps, like me, you think of abandonment, abuse, or neglect? Maybe you think passive or uninterested? Controlling and judgmental?

In my experience, after forty years of ministry and counselling, I agree with many psychologists and criminologists that children who commit the most violent-impulsive crimes come from divorced homes, single-parent families, and broken, fatherless families.

The revised thinking is that family breakdown feeds social illnesses. Rich or poor, white or black, the children of divorce and those born outside of wedlock struggle through life at a measurable disadvantage.

We are in the midst of a fatherless epidemic. Fathers have exited the picture; they have died in war or not returned home. Children grow up in families with unstable walls and cracked foundations. They have been left to battle the storms of life without the provision they need, the protection of a real man, a real, loving father. Not to mention no father to promote them into their destinies.

I know people who have incredibly blessed relationships with their fathers. But sadly, in my experience, they are the minority. I hear many stories of people who feel abandoned, devalued, criticized, and unable to measure up. I have heard stories of horrible abuse and dads who were never really "there." Yet, as important as a dad is, many children on this planet live without a father or bear the scars of an abusive, demanding, uninvolved father.

We are the seeds of our fathers: We come into life and settle into our created identities; we confront the parts of us that are like our fathers, both desirable and undesirable. It makes no difference if our memories of them are positive or negative; we are forever connected to our biological fathers. Whether our fathers were good men and lived up to their duties or scoundrels and neglected responsibility, it does not matter. We remain the product of their seed.

Today the dominant global culture is that of fatherlessness. This culture is subtle and pervasive, teaching people to think like orphans. Orphans have no protection or provision besides what they can create for themselves and must struggle for survival by whatever means necessary. Today's fatherless culture directly conflicts with the culture of the Kingdom of God. Within the culture of the Kingdom of God is the family of God. The Kingdom of God is the base of authority and rule that empowers His house in both domains. The traditional family structure has changed to where children are deprived of rich, meaningful relationships with their fathers, even when they are alive or physically present. When parents are lost to disease, children become the heads of households, responsible for raising and caring for their younger siblings. They are orphans raising orphans.

Today's greatest challenge for men, especially young men, is that they suffer from an identity crisis. An identity doesn't come from a gang, the government, or books. It comes from a father. A man must be affirmed by a father to confirm his manhood. They lack the nurturing influence of a true father to give them identity.

"DAD is destiny!" These words jumped off the pages of a US News & World Report page, and it amazed me that the secular world can have this profound revelation! They wrote, "One of the greatest challenges of this world is to restore the male crisis facing most communities. The key to restoring and preserving a sane and healthy society is the salvation of the male, especially as a responsible father."[1]

Good or bad, present or passive, Dad defines us. He shapes what we become, how we think, how we act, how we feel about ourselves, and how we respond to others.

Depending on how you were treated, mistreated, or just plain ignored, you have come up with your own ideas of what a father is like. How your father behaved toward you, what he said to you, how he treated you, and everything he did and didn't do influenced you somehow. Because of this, I am convinced that your relationship with your earthly dad has also affected and distorted how you see and perceive your heavenly Father, God.

Many people wonder, "Is God a bigger version of my dad? Would He leave me if I fail or punish me for not measuring up?"

Some of you might be thinking of a dad who expected more than you could ever give or more than you could ever be. I have friends—successful business people and Church leaders—who are still trying to please that kind of father. Perhaps your father loved you but never disciplined you. Or, hopefully, your dad was loving and amazing!

Regardless of your answer, I think that whatever comes to mind when you think about your father, there is a good chance that you attribute similar characteristics to your image of your heavenly Father. Simply put, your image of God has been subconsciously formed and shaped by the father figures in your life.

Some would say you do not desire a close relationship with God. Your image of God may be so distorted that you have abandoned the possibility of forming any connection with Him. I hope your image of God will be clearer and brighter tomorrow than today, and your relationship with Him will be stronger. God has revealed Himself through His creation, and you can see evidence of Him all around. He has also revealed Himself in each of our hearts. The Bible tells us in **Ecclesiastes 3:11 (NKJV), "Yet God has made everything beautiful for its own time. He has planted eternity in the human heart, but people cannot see the whole scope of God's work from beginning to end."** The ultimate revelation of God as a loving Father came to us through the cross, death and resurrection of His Son, Jesus Christ.

Many people get irritated and even angry when talking about God as a Father. We call them spiritual orphans—hurt, lonely, confused, and separated. They tend to see God through the lens of their own experiences, and when those experiences have been hurtful, it contributes to a false impression of God. Fathers who rejected their children, didn't talk to them and

4

ignored them have caused their children to have a distorted view of God.

Most of the people we have gotten to know in the past thirty years, whom we have pastored and counselled, came from homes with an absent or dysfunctional father. What is meant by an absent father? Whether a father is dead, absent due to divorce, absent because of work, absent through ignorance and carelessness about showing love and affection, or absent as a result of his own dysfunctional withdrawal from everybody, the outcome is still the same for children! It can destroy their lives! In fact, it destroys their identities, as one of the primary responsibilities of fathers is to develop their children's identities. Mainly, absent fathers can ruin their children's sexual identities, as one of the primary roles of a father is the development of this area of their child's life.

Most people are raised without a loving, stable father. Most cultures have been forced to accept the lifestyle of absent fathers, even embracing motherhood as a higher position than the role of a father.

None of our fathers are always completely bad. For, in the worst of us, there is always something good! Even the worst fathers in the world have some good qualities! But most people in the world are raised without an active father.

We all know Father's Day is far less celebrated than Mother's Day worldwide. An interesting story took place in a prison in South America. One Mother's Day, the prison decided to make a special event for the occasion. Many prisoners got involved and made gifts for their mothers, and the day was a huge success. Then, when the authorities tried to do the same thing for Father's Day, it turned out to be a complete failure. None of the inmates participated because most didn't have a father.

Sadly, we see that among our African indigenous people, where most children are raised without an actively involved father. That is our observation, ministering in Africa and counselling many of our students and Church members.

My observation of school children in South Africa and the rest of Africa is that very few of them still have their original fathers at home. Most of these children live in homes without a father's presence. Their grandmothers or other family raises many African children.

Observing the significant number of young people in prisons, it seems to be that young people commit most of all violent-impulsive crimes. These wounded young people addicted to all kinds of drugs are the product of a generation whose philosophy is privatism, materialism, and hedonism. Many parents denied God, moral absolutes, and the importance of the family.

Unfortunately, the Church has often reinforced the orphan mentality and the fatherless culture. The Church should be a father to the fatherless and reveal the Father to the fatherless.

An abusive or indifferent father alienates his children, often resulting in anger toward the father and depression among the children. Abuse comes in different forms, and it can be violent or nonviolent. And nonviolent abuse has been known to be as effective as physical abuse in alienating a child. Hard and humiliating words can destroy children's views of themselves, resulting in a profound sense of rejection. A silent or uninvolved father communicates to the child that the child's interests are of no particular value to the father. Therefore, the child is unimportant, and they often feel that their existence is of no value.

Whether we like it or not, mothers have become the dominant cultural influence upon succeeding generations. Mothers have been left to raise children alone, which is not how it should be. The fatherless generation is disconnected from their fathers' traditions and views them with suspicion. The father's role is to confirm the child's identity and impart a sense of purpose and destiny.

Adam's original mandate was to represent his Father. Although he sinned and his rule increasingly deviated from his original mandate, God never revoked the authority He gave Adam over creation. When God placed Adam on the earth, He accurately positioned Adam as the head of the government of Heaven's Kingdom in the earth domain. The attack upon Adam by satan was targeted to disrupt the accuracy of his position.

God is love, and He expressed His love by creating man. Love is inherently vulnerable. It is risky, as it puts one's interests in the hands of another while investing faith and hope in the reciprocal affection of the other. The full expression of God's love is meant to occur corporately, with each individual being one facet of the larger expression. This corporate expression is built upon the father-and-son relationship. This relationship is the building block of the Family of God, also known as the House of God.

God decided to create man (Adam) as His Son, and man was powerless in this decision. The love of God for man is the foundation for man's purpose in creation. When man separated himself from his father through sin, his purpose in creation was lost for a season. Just as a son needs a father to understand his identity and purpose properly, a father requires a son to display the father's nature. The Son (Jesus) radiates God's glory and the exact representation of His being.

Overwhelming evidence supports the notion that there are specific emotional and psychological needs only a male can provide to children. Likewise, there are unique needs that only a female can meet for her children.

Jesus came to fix man's problem of fatherlessness. Many fathers are estranged from their children. Many homes are without fathers. Before Christ, Adam's children, throughout the ages, knew little about the Father because they were born fatherless as a result of Adam's sin and rejection of Him.

Jesus knew the Father and became the Source and Progenitor of a new race of fathers-those who know their heavenly Father through His Son. You cannot be a true father unless you have one yourself. The only person in history qualified to father us who knew the Father, and that person is Jesus.

The most outstanding example of a father's critical role was demonstrated in Jesus's life. He spoke of His Father more than anyone else. He expressed and emphatically confessed His need, dependency, and submission to His Father at every opportunity. He never hesitated to give credit to His Father for any activity or success, thereby confirming the sustaining work of God in His life. He saw His Father as the Source, Resource, and Purpose for His entire life. (John 8:19, John 8:26–29, John 8:38, John 8:49, John 14:8–11, John 20:21)

[1] Joseph P. Shapiro, Joannie M. Schrof, Mike Tharp, and Dorian Friedman, "Honor Thy Children" U.S.News & World Report, February 27, 1995.

Feeling sorry for yourself or bitter about your absent or abusive father will not help you become whole and dynamic or the person God has made you to be. Surrender to the Holy Spirit's healing and restoration.

2. THE FATHERLESS CHURCH

If Moses accepted a father figure in his life at eighty, and Joshua acknowledged Moses as his father at eighty, what is our excuse? If a mature and grown-up man at eighty can realise he needs a father, then we are without excuse.

This chapter refers to the need for spiritual fathers within the Church who are present and available for spiritual sons.

The previous revival movements of God within His Church, like the Pentecostal and Charismatic, focused on giftings and ministry of the Spirit. But the present move of God, in His Church all over the world, focuses on God building His House (His Church) with spiritual fathers and sons. It is now all about Heaven's family on Earth. This is a movement beyond petty doctrine and building empires. God is Family. His Kingdom is family! He is restoring a healthy Church Family.

Many Churchgoers (Christians) still have no or little relationship with God, our ABBA Father. And so, they do not necessarily visibly represent our heavenly ABBA Father within the local Church. The Roman Catholic Church and some other Sacramental Churches call their leaders 'Father' or 'Pope' (Latin for father, Papa). Unfortunately, this is not a formula to restore or reflect the image of Father God here on earth. With the absent father syndrome in this world and the Church, we must do far more than that to fulfil God's ultimate plan for His Church.

Churches without spiritual fathers are not necessarily wrong or less effective, but they are still incomplete. Very few Churches operate as heavenly families on earth, and very few are known for being a father-led movement. We believe that one of the primary callings of the Church is to reveal our heavenly Father to this fatherless generation. We need real, anointed spiritual fathers in every Church and ministry for that to happen.

"Where have all the fathers gone?"

My over forty-five years of involvement with different kinds of Churches has taught me one main thing regarding the Body of Christ: In most churches, there are almost no real spiritual fathers. If there are some, I don't know of them. I will be very pleased and grateful to acknowledge them!

If I may add what Paul the apostle said in **1 Corinthians 4:15 (NKJV); "For though you might have ten thousand instructors (mentors) in Christ, yet *you do* not *have* many fathers; for in Christ Jesus, I have begotten you (I have become your father) through the gospel."**

My experiences with so-called spiritual fathers have made me realise that the lack of Godly (Fatherly) character has robbed the Church of real apostolic fathers carrying the heart and character of God, our ABBA Father.

In the past, I connected to some strong leaders just to realise that although these leaders are powerful preachers and organisers, they are not necessarily anointed, spiritual fathers. I have experienced more abuse and humiliation at the hands of these leaders while trying to find a spiritual father who knows how to mobilise and empower me as a spiritual son.

When Moses was forty years old, living in the house of Pharaoh, he could have anything he wanted. Yet, God sent him to Midian to Jethro, and He kept him there for forty years, and Jethro became his father. Moses was already an educated man with a degree in almost every subject of those times. But Moses never had a father who fathered him, and a nation cannot experience deliverance without the spirit of fathering.

Moses could not be a revolutionary leader who would instigate a revolution and uprising to set two million people free. Moses first had to develop the spirit of fathering, he got that from Jethro, and it took forty years to impart that to him.

Moses received the counsel of his father, Jethro. If Moses, at eighty, accepted a father figure in his life, and Joshua acknowledged Moses as his father at eighty, what is our excuse? If a mature and grown-up man at eighty can realise he needs a father, then we are without excuse. We need fathers and guidance as well.

King Saul in the Old Testament is an excellent example of a strong leader who did not understand fathering the upcoming generation. Saul's father was an absent army general. He manipulated his son Jonathan and tried to kill David, knowing that David would become the next King. His heart was filled with jealousy, fear, and inferiority.

Why would the New Testament Church still not understand and not acknowledge this truth? Why are they not developing the grace gifting of spiritual fathers in the Body of Christ after two thousand years of existence? The answer is partially known: Spiritual fathers are called and anointed by God, and secular denominational structures, which most Church movements adhere to, will not (or cannot) create or produce the ministry of fathers to spiritual sons. I say this according to the definition of spiritual fathers, which I will explain throughout the rest of the book.

In a closer study of the type of spiritual father Paul referred to in 1 Corinthians 4:15, we realise that this kind of father has an apostolic anointing, which is first among the five-fold ministry leadership giftings mentioned in Ephesians 4:11–16. Sadly, many Churches do not believe in this kind of apostolic leadership ministry.

Most Churches, Church networks, and denominations are "electing" leaders into positions and calling them chairmen, secretaries, and other secular names.

The Church has different leadership structures; some may be more Biblical than others. However, many leadership structures are founded on secular, worldly thinking and opinions, and we seldom find Biblical leadership functions like those of Ephesians 4:12 – 16 in any movement.

The Church has been mostly mothered and not fathered!

The reformation of 500 years ago has partially restored the Church. It has taken it from a legalistically mothering pastoral system to a restoration of the Spirit of the Father that breathed New Testament discipleship back to its original intention.

Because the role and ministry of spiritual fathers has been ignored and resisted for most of the history of the Church, we have been raising a dysfunctional fatherless Church.

The Bible is clear; the Church's foundation must be apostles and prophets. They are the leaders of the leaders, the fathers of the family of God. **Ephesians 2:20 NKJV "having been built on the foundation of the apostles and prophets, Jesus Christ Himself being the chief corner*stone*".**

Churches that believe that the apostolic and prophetic ministry is still for today, and allow these ministries to be developed and acknowledged, are the Churches that see the Spirit of Father emerging among the leaders.

Because most traditional Church systems only allow the ministry of the 'pastor' to care for the people of God and to lead the Church to be a healthy and dynamic organism (movement), the Church may become weak and poor. It may lack the fatherly leadership that brings health and balance to the Body of Christ.

Unbiblical operating systems

We know now that healthy fathers in a family bring order, discipline, vision, security and healthy love relationships. The Church has many unbiblical operating systems and structures because of the absence of spiritual fathers. Unlike the Kingdom of Heaven's family system, I call it unbiblical because they are secular, worldly systems.

Here are a few examples of some of the implementations of operating systems within Churches.

Pyramid hierarchical system

This is seen in the Roman Catholic Churches and other sacramental Churches. The Pope is the highest order and has more authority than the Word of God. The Pope and his Bishops make decisions and rules for the rest of the Church.

Presbyterian system

The Elders (and sometimes the Deacons) rule. It operates as a Church board or an Elders' board. Very close to a Secular semi-democratic system. It does not represent or acknowledge the five-fold ministries of Ephesians 4. In many Churches, it controls the Church and the Pastor.

Congregational system

The people rule the pastor! The members of the Church rule! This is a worldly secular democratic system.

Pastoral system

The pastor rules as an individual and even as a dictator. He may draw some close friends in for advice.

Cell Church and Home Churches

The lack of leadership in these groups causes nobody and everybody to rule! This model can be very effective and healthy if every small group is connected to anointed elders and apostolic leaders.

Denominations

This kind of Church is built around doctrine and belief systems. If your doctrine is not 100% according to the denomination's law book, then you are out and cut off from fellowship. This is seldom a relationship-based family system.

Networking

Networks usually operate leaderless and fragmented; most of the time, they seldom last for many years.

Para Church Movements

Many para-Church movements are doing great work worldwide, reaching more lost people than most Churches. They replace the ministry to the broken world that the Church should do, like most mission societies or mercy and welfare ministries. It would be great if the local Churches became part of all these outreach ministries, and as such, the 'para-Church' movements would empower the Church in missions and outreach.

'Orphanage assemblies' led by spiritual nurses

These Churches are without spiritual fathers and are led by immature pastoral leaders. Because of the weak leadership, the people become like orphans and enslaved people. Sonship is not demonstrated or cultivated. It is like an orphanage led by spiritual nurses.

A Dream come true!

What could your ultimate blessing in discipleship and spiritual growth be?

Suppose you can have a healthy, mature, earthly spiritual father who cheers you on to fulfil your divine calling! It would be like Father God Himself taking your hand and leading and encouraging you to become what He made you to be!

3. THE ELIJAH GENERATION

Malachi 4: 5 – 6 (NKJV)

"Behold, I will send you Elijah the prophet before the coming of the great and dreadful day of the Lord. And he will turn the hearts of the fathers to the children, and the hearts of the children to their fathers, lest I come and strike the earth with a curse."

About twenty-five hundred years ago, the biblical prophet Malachi spoke of the work and purpose of the coming Messiah by declaring this powerful word. We are living in the days of Elijah. Crucial to this mantle is the turning of the hearts of the fathers to the children and the hearts of the children to the fathers.

These two Scripture verses are the final verses of the Old Testament. These words are the focal point of an entire era of revelation. The message of all forty books in more than half of our bible reaches an apex at these verses. More than two thousand years of God's relationship with humankind ends in these sentences. The entire age of kings and prophets culminates in these words. These two verses contain prophecy, a promise of blessing and the threat of a curse simultaneously. The promise of blessing is that the relationship between fathers and sons will be restored. Without turning hearts, the following will be released, "the earth will be smitten with a curse".

The scripture from Malachi demands a wineskin of intimacy and relationship between leadership and disciples, between fathers and sons. This expects the dismantling of the traditional Church's clergy-laity institutional model, which does not transmit grace, family life or this significant heavenly connection of father and sons in unity and harmony. The 'father-son' model, which is not gender-based, demands intimacy and a sustained lifelong relationship with the spiritual son. This might mean the father cannot be fired, retrenched, transferred or retired. Only death separates the relationship.

The implication is that the divine assessment of man's fundamental problem is a fatherless problem. Because of no fathers, we have no real mature sons. This is what Jesus came to restore. This is the prophetic call of Malachi 4, expecting the Elijah generation, that is the Jesus generation, to bring the family back to God's Church.

Millions of Jewish descendants still keep the Passover feast. The feast time is used to remember past blessings and look forward to future events on God's timetable. Every year at their Passover celebration, the table setting includes one place for Elijah's coming. An extra glass of wine and a plate are set aside; no one can use them. Abraham's children are taught to expect Elijah to come. Unfortunately, most also missed or ignored the coming of the second Elijah (John the Baptist announcing the coming of the Messiah) and of Jesus Christ Himself!

Does the Church have a place ready for Elijah?

As Christians who are followers of the complete revelation of God. Do we have a setting for Elijah to return and be welcomed? Both times when Elijah or the spirit of Elijah came before, the leaders of God's people found no place for him. Will the Church receive him now? Are we any better than our fathers? Elijah came first in the days of Ahab (1 Kings 17). The spirit of Elijah came in the person of John the Baptist, who prepared the way of the Lord Jesus Christ.

LUKE 1:17 (NKJV) "He will also go before Him in the spirit and power of Elijah, 'to turn the hearts of the fathers to the children,' and the disobedient to the wisdom of the just, to make ready a people prepared for the Lord."

The Spirit of Elijah is the Holy Spirit operating through the Church of this generation, the end-time Church, to build out Heaven's operational system; Father (ABBA), His sons and spiritual fathers and sons. Remember that the term 'son' is a non-gender word for daughters and sons.

This book is an urgent call for the obeying and restoration of theology and interpretation regarding the coming of Elijah and the promise of a blessing for obedience and a warning of a potential curse for ignorance.

(Malachi 4: 5–6) These two Scripture verses are the final verses of the Old Testament. These words are the focal point of an entire era of revelation. The height and apex of all forty books in over half of our Bible suddenly stopped at these verses. More than two thousand years of God's relationship with humankind ends in these sentences. The entire age of kings and prophets culminates in these words. It is all about what the Jesus generation must accomplish!

4. GOD IS A MULTIGENERATIONAL GOD, OPERATING ON EARTH AS A FAMILY WITH FATHERS AND SONS

Fathers build legacies for generations to come.

God called many fathers to be part of His legacy through the ages. Beginning with Adam, the son of God, He built many generations through time to bless the earth. Specifically, fathers such as Abraham, who He called and sent, after him Isaac, then Jacob and the twelve tribes until Jesus was born. Then, in the new testament, this generational blessing primarily becomes a spiritual family of fathers and sons.

God built a generation from Adam, the son of God, and He called many to be part of His generation to bless the earth. Specifically, Abraham was called and sent, then Isaac, Jacob, and the twelve tribes until Jesus was born. Then in the New Testament, the generation of blessing primarily becomes a spiritual family of fathers and sons.

Heaven is family! The Kingdom of God is family! God revealed Himself as a three-fold family of Godliness: Father, Son and Holy Spirit. The Church is called to be a family of families.

Proverbs 13:22 (NKJV) "A good *man* leaves an inheritance to his children's children, But the wealth of the sinner is stored up for the righteous."

Our Heavenly Father sees the beginning from the end, and those who bear the Father's heart must see generationally. If we understand that the father's sins are passed on to the third and fourth generation (see Exod. 34:6–7; Deut. 5:9–10), we must recognize that blessing also must be passed on to the third and fourth generation. True fathers speak to their sons and daughters, their children's sons and daughters, and their grandchildren's sons and daughters. What a father does and says will bring about a legacy that the Father in Heaven has desired to establish with Adam and Eve since the beginning.

I have come to understand that the size of the ministry does not measure success, but what you have developed for the next generation does. It is not determined by what you have built but by what you have helped others to build.

Heaven's operating system on Earth: A Family with Fathers and Sons

Heaven is family; Father, Son and Holy Spirit. Heaven has been downloaded into God's creation, making men (fathers), women (mothers) and children. Healthy families are the perfect image of God displayed as Father, Holy Spirit and children. God made man a reflection of Heaven on Earth. Through Jesus, God builds His Church to be a spiritual family. Every born-again child of God can now belong to God's family. God is raising fathers and mothers in God's family to bring God's people to maturity!

The New Testament starts with a list of fathers and sons to explain the lineage of blessings from which Jesus was born.

The Old Testament ends with a promise and warning that if fathers' and sons' relationships and legacy are not restored, a curse will be activated on the earth. The promise is in the prophetic truth of the coming of the spirit of Elijah, which culminates in the coming of Jesus the Messiah, who will restore everything! We are ultimately the Elijah generation!

Malachi 4:5–6 (NKJV) "Behold, I will send you Elijah the prophet before the coming of the great and dreadful day of the Lord. And he will turn The hearts of the fathers to the children, And the hearts of the children to their fathers, lest I come and strike the earth with a curse."

The Kingdom of God should be growing in multiplication. This happens when fathers impart their spirit to their sons.

God is a multi-generational God. He sees far beyond one generation. We see only our lives, but He sees much further.

I have long understood that a spiritual son's destiny has been entwined in his spiritual father's passion, just as his future was indeed entwined in his spiritual father's future.

Adam and Eve were released into their destiny when God spoke the Word over them. Man's destiny was to subdue the earth and have dominion. But first, man was instructed to do something vital to achieve this goal. Man was instructed to "be fruitful and multiply."

"And the things that you have heard from me among many witnesses, commit these to faithful men who will be able to teach others also." 2 Timothy 2:2 (NKJV).

Here, Paul writes to his spiritual son, Timothy, saying the same thing. Paul writes to his son Timothy to impart to Timothy's spiritual sons who will impart to their sons! Observe that this short verse has no less than four generations of believers.

The last chapter of the book of Job is like a prophetic revelation of our apostolic season and the lifestyle we are supposed to experience: From a curse to a blessing, four generations of sons of inheritance, a generation of a double blessing and a restoration of everything the previous generations have lost.

Job 42:10–17 (NKJV); "And the LORD restored Job's losses when he prayed for his friends. Indeed, the LORD gave Job twice as much as he had before. Now the LORD blessed the latter *days* of Job more than his beginning; for he had fourteen thousand sheep, six thousand camels, one thousand yokes of oxen, and one thousand female donkeys. He also had seven sons and three daughters. And he called the name of the first Jemimah, the name of the second Keziah, and the name of the third Keren-Happuch. In all the land were found no women *so* beautiful as the daughters of Job; and their father gave them an inheritance among their brothers. After this, Job lived one hundred and forty years and saw his children and grandchildren *for* four generations. So Job died, old and full of days."

The challenge to all of us and to the Church, in general, is to become a legacy of heavenly blessings for all generations, godly anointed fathers producing powerful spiritual sons for many generations.

5. BIBLICAL EXAMPLES OF FATHERLESS CHILDREN AND FAILED FATHERS

No father is totally perfect, and no single child is totally dysfunctional. No bad father is totally evil, and every dysfunctional father definitely has some good characteristics. Some 'evil' areas still need more healing and deliverance in the best of us!

Most fathers in the Old and New Testaments failed in many ways. Every father I placed in the 'failed' character group has some positive characteristics. That is why we need salvation and empowerment through Jesus Christ.

Following are a few examples of failed fathers and children who were not well-fathered:

Adam and sons

We don't know why the firstborn child of Adam and Eve turns out to be a rebellious and inferior young man. His murderous character caused him to be the first to be cursed after Eden's failure. Somehow his father, Adam, was not there to resolve the rebellion and deception of his firstborn.

Noah and sons

Although the building of the ark and the close fellowship within the ark gave us the impression that Noah's family operated very well as a family unit, Ham's disrespect was revealed by dishonouring his father in a moment of weakness. Noah's one mistake destroyed one of his sons and his descendants. Somehow Noah's relationship with this Son was not solid, and the result was that Ham's descendants, Canaan, were placed under a further curse because of their father's inability to honour Noah.

Abraham and Ishmael

Abraham had a great promise from God about his descendants and future family. He succeeded in so many things God asked of him but failed in this one thing to wait for the seed of promise, Isaac, who would be his real legacy and the carrier of the promises of God. According to the Bible, Abraham followed his own unbelieve and created a boy named Ismael from one of his slave women, and missed God's number one plan for him.

Isaac and Jacob & Esau

Isaac's twin sons, Esau and Jacob, were wrongly favoured by the two parents, who eventually caused a greater breakdown in their relationships. Jacob stole Esau's rights of the firstborn, and his mother helped him deceive their father and Esau.

Laban and Leah, and Rachel

What Jacob did to his brother happened to him. Laban deceived and trapped him by giving him the wrong wife and daughter. Laban's daughters had to lie to their dad, leaving him permanently to be with their husband.

Jacob and sons

Brothers want to kill brothers, and Jacob's inability to manage his twelve sons caused much pain and strife. Jacob favouring his sons Joseph and Benjamin, drove a lot of jealousy and hatred from the other ten sons. The positive result was that the twelve tribes were born out of this dysfunctional family after God restored much of their tension.

Eli and sons

As we look at Eli's relationship with his two biological sons, we discover that they were worthless. **"12 Now the sons of Eli *were* corrupt (worthless); they did not know the Lord." 1 Samuel 2:12 (NKJV).**

God has a plan and a purpose. It is not complicated. He simply wants us to be fruitful, multiply and subdue the earth. This is the true essence of a functional Kingdom. However, if we cannot hear God and be a living example, how can we impart anything to our sons and daughters? Eli didn't teach his sons nor impart his ability to hear God.

Eli's two sons were worthless, useless, and corrupt. They were dysfunctional and hopeless men because they did not know God. They practised religious rituals but did not know the pathways to the Father.

Samuel and sons

Samuel was a priest and prophet of Israel, revered for his wisdom and courage. However, he apparently learned his poor parenting skills from Eli, the Hi-priest, when he served the Lord in the temple at Shiloh. Samuel's sons behaviour was similarly as corrupt as Eli's was. As Samuel aged, he repeated Eli's error and appointed his own dishonourable sons to succeed him. Like Eli's sons, they were greedy and corrupt (1 Sam. 8:1–3).

Why David was a weak father?

1. His father, Jesse, did not acknowledge him as a worthy son. He did not think David had the potential to be the future King. Maybe, as the youngest child, David felt rejected and developed a faulty image of how a father and son should relate.

2. It seems that David and his father did not have an intimate relationship.

3. King Saul became David's new father. As a young man, David was taken into the house of Saul just to eventually experience Saul's jealous, dysfunctional, and murderous character. Many times Saul tried to kill David. For nearly fifteen years, David had to hide for his life.

4. David connects to Samuel the prophet and relates to him as a spiritual father and counsellor. He hid in the mountains from King Saul for fifteen years while Samuel was helping and motivating David.

1 Samuel 19:18 (NKJV) So David fled and escaped, and went to Samuel at Ramah, and told him all that Saul

had done to him. And he and Samuel went and stayed in Naioth

5. David did not resolve conflict, communicate, or show intimate love with his children. He failed to protect his daughter Tamar from being raped by her brother. He failed to discipline his son for what he had done to his sister. He failed to face Absalom and all the other children.

6. After David's sin with his neighbour's wife, the prophet Nathan came to him to announce God's discipline. David repented and showed remorse, and changed his behaviour radically.

7. A new season in his life started. According to the first few chapters of Proverbs, David's relationship with his son, Solomon from Bathsheba, changed his behaviour as a father radically. His way of raising Solomon became a new Godly journey.

Solomon and son

Although Solomon was seen as the wisest man ever to live, he failed with his son, who was supposed to follow him in leadership. Solomon did not follow his own wise words about serving God and loving other women, which eventually destroyed his own life! Solomon's son and successor, Rehoboam, ill-advisedly adopted a harsh policy toward the northern tribes, which seceded and formed their own kingdom of Israel. This left the descendants of Solomon with the southern kingdom of Judah.

Hezekiah

Hezekiah started so well, just to finish in a mess! God healed him from terminal sickness and gave him fifteen more years to live. During the extra fifteen years, he turned his back on God! His son Manasseh became one of the worst kings ever seen in Israel,

2 Chronicles 29:1–3 "Hezekiah became king *when he was* twenty-five years old, and he reigned twenty-nine years in Jerusalem. His mother's name *was* Abijah, the daughter of Zechariah. And he did *what was* right in the sight of the Lord, according to all that his father David had done. In the first year of his reign, in the first month, he opened the doors of the house of the Lord and repaired them."

2 Kings 20:1 ' In those days Hezekiah was sick and near death. And Isaiah the prophet, the son of Amoz, went to him and said to him, "Thus says the Lord: 'Set your house in order, for you shall die, and not live.' "'

After the prayers and petition of Hezikiah toward God, the prophet Isaiah brought the good news that God had mercy on him and gave him fifteen more years to live.

In 2 Chronicles 32:31, we saw God withdraw from him because his heart turned away from God.

2 Kings 20:16–19 'Then Isaiah said to Hezekiah, "Hear the word of the Lord: 'Behold, the days are coming when all that *is* in your house, and what your fathers have accumulated until this day, shall be carried to Babylon; nothing shall be left,' says the Lord. 'And they shall take away some of your sons who will descend from you, whom

28

you will beget, and they shall be eunuchs in the palace of the king of Babylon.' " So Hezekiah said to Isaiah, "<u>The word of the Lord which you have spoken *is* good</u>!" For he said, "Will there not be peace and truth at least in my days?"'

After God told him, He would destroy everything he had. He said, "It is good!". What a pathetic response! He actually said, "I don't care! You can kill my sons and destroy everything I have."

And the fruit of his disobedient life was his son ruling the nation, who was seen as one of the worst rulers in Israel's history.

6. BIBLICAL EXAMPLES OF SUCCESSFUL FATHERS AND CHILDREN

David and Solomon

The Bible has numerous examples of failed fathers but nearly no good examples of any successful fathers!

One of the few good examples is King David's later years with his son Solomon, son of Bathsheba. David passed the baton of being an anointed King on to Solomon, his son – one of the very few generational blessings. From our New Testament perspective, Solomon represents the Church of Jesus Christ. Solomon is seen as the wealthiest and wisest person ever to have lived. He built the perfect temple and ruled with majesty and authority. His counsel and wisdom had no limits, and his government's increase seemed unlimited. David and Solomon are a great prophetic picture of the Church and God's Kingdom. If we can accept that David wrote the first few chapters of the book of Proverbs, it reflects a very close and intimate relationship between them.

Despite what David told Solomon about women, Solomon allowed his love for women to destroy his last years, and his kingdom was eventually divided.

Joseph, Jesus' father, and siblings

Although we do not have much information about Joseph, the father of Jesus, we can evaluate the fruit of his influence in the life of his children. Joseph was obedient to God and was willing to protect his adopted firstborn. We know he was a well-known carpenter, and perhaps Jesus, as the oldest son, spent much time building furniture and working with wood. We do not have much information about Joseph's life, and we suspect Joseph died during Jesus's young adulthood.

Jesus's brother James became one of the apostolic leaders of the Church in Jerusalem. See Acts 15:13–21 where James took the lead during the Jerusalem meeting. His other brothers and sisters also appeared to have become followers of Jesus and were active in the Church in Jerusalem.

John the Baptist

His father was a high priest serving God and his family. After encountering God in the Holy of Holies, he and his wife raised their son, John, to fulfil his special calling from God. We know that John's parents raised him well because of his life's fruit and dedication. God called him to prepare the way for the Lord Jesus Christ. He was seen as one of the most powerful prophets in the entire Bible. **Luke 7:28 (NKJV) "For I say to you, among those born of women there is not a greater prophet than John the Baptist, but he who is least in the Kingdom of God is greater than he."**

7. KNOWING THE CHARACTER OF ABBA FATHER

How do we know God as the Father?

1. Through the life of Jesus Christ:

   If you want to know the Father, study the Son! Jesus' primary purpose for coming to earth was to reveal the Father to this fatherless planet. John 17

2. Through the sons of God:

   The healthy relationships of God's spiritual sons reveal the love and character of God.

3. Through fathers:

   This applies to natural fathers and spiritual fathers. Fathers develop fathers, not only sons. Real sons have the potential to become powerful fathers to new sons. A man learns how to father from a father. A father grows in fatherhood by leaning on ABBA Father.

4. Through the living Word

   One of the most beautiful revelations in the Bible is that God is our Father. God reveals Himself in the Bible

32

as a gentle, forgiving Father, desiring to be intimately involved with each and every aspect of our lives. However, every person seems to have a different idea of God. That's because they subconsciously attach feelings and impressions of their earthly father or other authority figures to their understanding of their Heavenly Father. Good experiences bring us closer to knowing and understanding God, just as bad experiences create distorted pictures of our Father's love for us. Paul twice mentions that the Holy Spirit in us calls out 'ABBA Father'. ABBA is Hebrew for Daddy and reflects the very intimate relationship expected between Father and us. Do you know Father as your Daddy? Do you have the intimate Name of Father, ABBA, on your lips?

Some qualities and characteristics the Bible teaches about Father God

Creator

One who creates us in His image, with the freedom to choose whether or not to respond to His love. **Isaiah 64:8 (NKJV) "But now, O Lord, You are our Father; We are the clay, and You our potter; And all we are the work of Your hand."**

Provider

One who loves to provide for our physical, emotional, mental, and spiritual needs. **Matthew 7:11 (NKJV) "If you then, being evil, know how to give good gifts to your children, how much more will your Father who is in heaven give good things to those who ask Him!"**

The greatest revelation and example of God as the Provider can be found in the story of the sacrifice of Isaac. There on the mountain, God revealed Himself as the Provider. Abraham believed that God would provide, and God honoured him with the miracle of provision. A ram was provided to be sacrificed in place of Abraham's son Isaac.

Healer

God's first revelation to His people coming out of Egypt was that He is the Healer!

Travelling out of the land of slavery to the promised land, God gave them the miracle of the Red Sea, opening up for them to travel through, where they saw their enemies drowning in the sea. Walking through the desert on their way to Mount Sinai, they came to a place of bitter water. God used this place to teach them the principles of divine life. God healed the water from bitterness to sweetness. A prophetic demonstration of applying the wood (the cross) to life's bitterness turns it into the sweet taste of God's goodness. That was the first time God introduced Himself to the Hebrew people as their Healer! God promised they would never have the sicknesses and diseases of Egypt in their lives.

Exodus 15:22–26 (NKJV) "So Moses brought Israel from the Red Sea; then they went out into the Wilderness of Shur. And they went three days in the wilderness and found no water. Now when they came to Marah, they could not drink the waters of Marah, for they *were* bitter. Therefore, the name of it was called Marah. And the people complained against Moses, saying, "What shall we drink?" So he cried out to the Lord, and the Lord showed him a tree. When he cast *it* into the waters, the waters were made sweet. There He made a statute and an ordinance

for them. There He tested them, and said, **"If you diligently heed the voice of the Lord your God and do what is right in His sight, give ear to His commandments and keep all His statutes, I will put none of the diseases on you which I have brought on the Egyptians. For I _am_ the Lord who heals you."**

Friend and counsellor

God the Father longs to have an intimate friendship with us and share wise counsel and instruction. **Isaiah 9:6 (NKJV) "For unto us a Child is born, unto us a Son is given; And the government will be upon His shoulder. And His name will be called Wonderful, Counselor, Mighty God, Everlasting Father, Prince of Peace."**

Corrector and discipline

God loves and therefore corrects and disciplines us. **Hebrews 12:5–6 (NKJV) "And you have forgotten the exhortation which speaks to you as to sons: "My son, do not despise the chastening of the Lord, nor be discouraged when you are rebuked by Him; For whom the Lord loves He chastens, And scourges every son whom He receives."**

Redeemer

God, the Father, is the One who forgives his children's faults and brings good out of their failures and weaknesses. **Psalms 103:12–13 (NKJV) "As far as the east is from the west,**

So far, has He removed our transgressions from us.

As a father pities his children, So the Lord pities those who fear Him."

Comforter

God cares for and promises to comfort us in time of need. **2 Corinthians 1:3–4 (NKJV) "Blessed *be* the God and Father of our Lord Jesus Christ, the Father of mercies and God of all comfort, who comforts us in all our tribulation, that we may be able to comfort those who are in any trouble, with the comfort with which we ourselves are comforted by God."**

Defender and deliverer

One who loves to protect, defend, and deliver his children. **Psalm 91:1–3 (NKJV) "He who dwells in the secret place of the Most High, shall abide under the shadow of the Almighty.**

I will say of the Lord, "*He is* my refuge and my fortress; My God, in Him I will trust." Surely He shall deliver you from the snare of the fowler *and* from the perilous pestilence."

Father

One who wants to free us from all false gods so that he can be a Father to us. **2 Corinthians 6:18 (NKJV) "I will be a Father to you, and you shall be My sons and daughters, says the Lord Almighty."**

Father of the fatherless

One who cares for the homeless and the widow. **Psalms 68:5–6 (NKJV) "A father of the fatherless, a defender of widows, is God in His holy habitation. God sets the solitary in families; He brings out those who are bound into prosperity; But the rebellious dwell in a dry land."**

Father of love

One who reveals himself to us and reconciles us to himself through Jesus Christ. **John 16:27 (NKJV) "for the Father Himself loves you, because you have loved Me, and have believed that I came forth from God."**

Remember these key principles for knowing God the Father:

- As the Source, God the Father had everything in Him before anything was. Everything that exists is in God.
- God is the Progenitor. He upholds and supports all that He created.
- Sin came from the first man-Adam-who turned his back on his Father.
- Salvation comes from the Man-Jesus, the Second Adam, providing us with the way to return to the Father.
- Jesus knew the Father and became the Source and Progenitor of a new race of fathers who know the Father through the Son.
- Fathers are progenitors. They birth generations after them that are like themselves and their forefathers. When God fathers a man, He produces godly fathers.
- Fathers are the source of instruction, information, and knowledge about God, the ultimate Source of all life.
- We learn how God disciplines, teaches, instructs and acts through an earthly father who embodies the Father.

8. THE ROLE AND CHARACTER OF REAL FATHERS

Principles of fatherhood

A principle is a fundamental law that governs function and behaviour. We must understand the basic laws of fatherhood in order to be effective fathers.

The father is the source, just as God is the Father of all living things and made man to be the father of the human family. Every man is created with the responsibility of fatherhood. Every male carries millions of sperm because he is the "source." God has prepared men to be fathers.

Fatherhood is God's way of building and sustaining the human family. He plans to fulfil His vision of the earth as an extension of His heavenly Kingdom. God accomplishes this by having males function as the foundation of their homes. This creates the environment for all those the father is responsible for to be protected, thereby giving them the freedom to grow and prosper as God intended.

Being a "father" is rooted in God's image because God is Father.

In the Old Testament, the Hebrew word for father is "ab". "Abba", meaning Daddy, comes from this word. In the New Testament, the Greek word for father is "pater". So, you have ab and abba in Old Testament Hebrew and pater in New Testament Greek.

What do "ab" and "pater" mean? These words denote fundamental concepts that include the following characteristics by which we should measure and train fathers. True fatherhood can be found within these twelve essential functions:

1. Reflecting our Heavenly Father's image
2. Progenitor is an Originator or a Founder
3. Source
4. Sustainer and Nourisher
5. Protector
6. Teacher
7. Disciplinarian
8. Leader
9. Head
10. Caring One
11. Supporter
12. Developer

The function and calling of "father" is the highest honour God bestows on men.

The highest principle of fatherhood is that fathers provide identity. The lack of godly identity is the leading cause of dysfunctional men.

The measure of a man's success is directly related to his effectiveness as a godly father, for which God is the ultimate standard and only true example.

The fatherlessness of men and women is the most significant source of sin and character dysfunction.

Jesus came to fix man's problem of fatherlessness. Salvation results from Jesus, the Second Adam, who has provided us with the way to return to the Father and our original identity in Him.

God has called men to be fathers, like He is, to turn the hearts of the children back to the fathers. Suppose you understand this principle and responsibility and apply it in your life. God will then answer your prayers for provision because He will father you, just as you father your family.

The level of closeness and intimacy your child refers to when describing their relationship with you measures your effectiveness as a father.

Fathers are progenitors, the source that generates, supports, and upholds the coming generations.

The only way for a man to discover and live out his inherent fatherhood nature in times of social change is to focus on his God-given purpose rather than those roles related to a particular culture or time in history.

When a man enters God's presence, he begins to function again. Man's ability to work reveals the potential God has placed within him. He was born with something "hidden" in him that should benefit the world. God doesn't give males the finished product but the raw material with which to cultivate.

Men are designed to guard, defend, and cover everything under their care and spheres of influence.

The male must know God's Word in order to teach the instructions God gave him.

As you start to focus on what real fathers do, you may feel overwhelmed and challenged. The good news is that God has already deposited the DNA and godly ability within every man to do and be what God expects from him.

Fathers train their children.

God has given fathers the responsibility to train and equip everyone under their care. When fathers train their children, they teach by example, enabling them to learn by imitation.

A father follows the example of their Heavenly Father and teaches his offspring to follow him. A godly father thus leads everyone to follow him to God.

Men cannot be fathers to children they are not present with or train children who are not by their side. A child is trained by observing what their father does, says, and decides in the real world.

Fathers discipline

To understand what it means for the father to be the one who disciplines, we must first realise that discipline is not punishment. Discipline takes teaching to the next level. It is one thing to teach a child, but correction and further instruction help to shape a child's character. Discipline, therefore, is training.

Fathers need to disciple their households by allowing their families to observe them operating in a godly manner and the power of the Holy Spirit.

"Train up a child in the way he should go, and when he is old, he will not depart from it." Proverbs 22:6 (NKJV). This instruction is speaking to fathers. Notice the application of this principle in **Ephesians (NKJV) 6:4: "And you, fathers, do not provoke your children to wrath, but bring them up in the training and admonition of the Lord."**

Again, I want to emphasise that discipline is not punishment rendered by an enraged father. Paul clearly warned, **"21 Fathers, do not provoke your children, lest they become discouraged." Colossians 3:21 (NKJV).**

Father as head and leader:

Heads and leaders are, first and foremost, servants like Christ. It is impossible to assume a position of leadership without first serving.

Fathers must have the mind of Christ (see 1 Corinthians 2:16), which includes the knowledge and wisdom to lead a family in the ways of God.

As the visionary, the father anticipates things before they happen and prepares and equips the family to face the future. Fathers discern and address the ongoing needs of their families.

Listening is a gift that fathers give to their families. When men listen, their listening tells their families they care for them.

A true father speaks the Word of God in the home. The family can hear God's voice through the father's voice.

A father doesn't dominate or control his house. He develops the potential of everyone in his home through his leadership.

Father as one who cares:

Like God the Father, a father cares by spending his time and energy anticipating what his wife and children will need next.

A man's job is a gift from God intended to help care for a man's family. When a father places more importance on his work than his family, he makes an idol out of his career and will bring ruin upon himself and his family.

Fathers must set the right priorities. A father who cares like God the Father thinks of his wife and children before his job.

Pastors and Church leaders should be prime examples of fathers caring for their families.

All Church leaders and members are to love their wives as Christ loved the Church. Anointed apostolic fathers (Apostolic leaders) must father pastors/leaders in the Body of Christ. The Church needs real spiritual fathers who are able and anointed to father God's people and leaders.

Responsibilities and actions of a father (Make this your vision and prayer):

- Reading and applying the Word of God.
- Praying and interceding.
- Making correct decisions based on the principles of God.
- Working in the real world, living out the example of dedication and hard work.
- Sharing the gospel with others.
- Openly worshipping and praising God the Father.
- Handling and solving problems without compromise.
- Being promise keepers and not promise breakers.

- Treating their wives with honour and dignity.
- Honouring others above themselves.
- Love their enemies.
- Make sure that their words and actions correspond.
- Fathers believe in their sons.
- Fathers help their sons to discover what they love.
- Fathers show their children how to love their wives.
- Father so loves the world that He sent His Son. Fathers send and bless their sons to be sent and to go into the world.
- Fathers provide and steward resources.
- Fathers treat every individual as unique and special. Don't treat sons (and daughters) equally but according to each one's calling and gifting. Remember, sameness isn't fairness.
- Fathers mobilise their sons further and higher than themselves.
- Fathers give identity and legacy.
- Fathers pay the price for their son's success.
- Fathers create a joyful, hopeful, and faithful culture.

A Summary of the Purpose of Fathers

- God created man to be a father like Himself, representing Him on earth and sustaining what comes from him.
- Out of man came the woman and marriage. Out of marriage came children and a family. Families create communities, and communities develop societies or nations. Therefore, fathers are the foundation of all cultures and nations.
- The Church cannot fix society's problems when the foundation is out of place.

- A father, like God, sustains, nourishes, and protects what comes out of him as the source, regardless of behaviour or how his provision is received.
- Men who are fathers, like the Father, are the unshakable foundation God purposed from the beginning when He created Adam.

9. BECOMING A SON OF ABBA FATHER

The Name of the Father on your forehead

In Revelations 13 and 14, we find a beautiful comparison between the mark of the beast and the mark of the Father.

In Revelation 13, the number 666 is the prophetic number of the beast. People of the world will wear this number on their foreheads and hands. Even nominal Christians may carry the mark of the beast.

Revelation 14:1 (NKJV) "Then I looked, and behold, a Lamb standing on Mount Zion, and with Him one hundred *and* forty-four thousand, having His Father's name written on their foreheads."

Let's break this scripture down. The forehead is the symbolic picture of man's mind, representing vision and mindset. Then, the one hundred and forty-four thousand is probably a symbolic mystery number of the genuine believers who know the Father. 144 is the sum of 12 multiplied by 12. The first twelve may represent the Old Testament believers, whereas the second 12 could represent the New Testament believers (which includes us). Lastly, 1000 is the number of perfection. So,12X12X1000 is the symbolic total number of believers when Jesus finally returns, and these believers will have the Name of the Father on their foreheads. That means you can only be called a son when you have the mind and name of the Father written on your forehead.

Our Identity As Sons

Much of the Body of Christ is caught up in an identity crisis. We have a secular view of God, absent of the full revelation of who we are. And without the full revelation of who we are, we are doomed to live our lives as spiritual orphans rather than manifest God's presence in our lives. Do we see God as a loving and just Father, or do we only see Him as a headmaster of an earthly orphanage, ready to crack the whip when we mess up? A loving and just Father will discipline us because of His love and wonderful plans for us. True sons know they depend on the Lord and acknowledge their need and direction, from their Heavenly Father, throughout the day. Those with an orphan mentality rely on their own ways and only seem to turn to Him when condemnation overwhelms them.

Living as Orphans

People who live by the law, who use it as a foundation of life, end up producing orphans. We call that dead religion! These people strive for praise, approval, and acceptance by following the rules. However, this only breeds insecurity and robs them of true peace. An orphan selfishly desires personal achievement to impress God and others. They often have no motivation to live a life of service in His Kingdom. Instead, they are driven by performance to impress Father and others and get acceptance.

Orphans feel they must be holier to earn God's love and acceptance. Unfortunately, this only produces feelings of shame and guilt. They often find comfort in addictions, counterfeit affections, compulsions, escapism, business, or tremendously popular "hyper-religious activities". Their self-image comes from their value, often based on their perceived comparisons with others. This is the foundation the enemy uses to birth false comforts.

Living as sons whose identity has been restored by the Father

Sons will live life while loving God and loving those around them. Sons will live a life of service motivated by deep love and gratitude for being unconditionally loved and accepted by their Heavenly Father. They find great joy and peace in the approval of their Heavenly Father. They are secure in God's love and justified by grace. They desire to be holy and do not want anything to hinder their intimate relationship with God.

Sons feel loved and affirmed because they know they are of tremendous value to their Father. Not because of what they do but because of who they are in Him. Their desire for obedience in a scriptural lifestyle is out of pleasure and delight in their Saviour rather than a sense of duty or trying to earn God's favour.

Sons find comfort in knowing the Father's character and often hearing His voice saying, "You are my beloved, and I have great joy in you ...". They will seek out intimate moments and times of divine downloads from the Father so that all their activity is Father-centred and to ensure that He orders all their steps.

To better understand the word 'son', we must first examine the Biblical usage of three Greek words. They are all found in Galatians 4:1–7, where Paul explains our position as sons. These three words are "napios", "teknon" and "huios." Though all three are sometimes translated as "son" or "child" in various translations, these three are very distinct.

Napios is the word for baby. Babies cannot do anything for themselves and are totally dependent on the people around them.

Teknon (John 1:12; 11:52; Romans. 8:16–17, 21; 9:8; Philippines 2:15; I John 3:1–2, 10) The Greeks usually used this word to speak of one who is a descendant by birth. In most instances, it is translated as "children" and often as a designation of believers in Christ. Christians are declared to be children of God (John 1:12; I John 3:1–2,10), having been born into His Family. John uses it exclusively this way. This word could actually be rendered "a born-one."

Huios (Matthew 5:9; Luke 20:36; Romans 8:14, 19; Galatians 3:26) The Greeks normally used this word to describe a relationship brought about by the legal action of adoption. The act of adoption was of great significance in the ancient Greek world. Paul's use of the word is placed within this context (the Greek word - huiothesia, meaning "the placing of sons," used in Romans 8:15; Galatians 4:5–7).

In the Western world, we think of adoption in terms of taking a child from one Family and making it a member of another. However, the Greek or Roman father adopted his own child as a son. Birth made him a child (teknon), but adoption made him a son (huios). There were stages of growth, education and discipline between birth and adoption. Only once maturity was reached was the child ready to be adopted into sonship. With adoption, the son was recognised as faithfully representing the father. He had arrived at the point of maturity where the father could entrust him to oversee the family business. Thus the son becomes the "heir" of his father's inheritance. Birth gives one the right to the inheritance, but adoption gives one participation in the inheritance.

"To be a son is infinitely more than being a child, and the terms are never loosely used by the Holy Spirit. The difference is not in a relationship but in a position. Every "born again" child of God has the nature of His Father and is a beloved member of His Father's Family. Adoption cannot make the child any nearer or dearer., However, it gives the child a status he did not previously enjoy, a position he did not occupy. It is his recognition as an adult son, attaining his maturity, and the seal upon his growth to maturity of mind and character. A child is born of God; a son is one taught of God. A child has God's nature; a son has God's character."

Jesus, the perfect Son, increased in favour and grace.

Isaiah 9:6 (NKJV) "For unto us a Child is born, unto us a Son is given; and the government will be upon His shoulder, and His name will be called Wonderful, Counsellor, Mighty God, Everlasting Father, Prince of Peace."

The Son is the essence, the very being, of the Father. The early Christians understood this. At the Council of Nicea (325 AD), they affirmed,

'We believe in one God, the Father almighty, maker of all things, visible and invisible; And in one Lord Jesus Christ, the Son of God, begotten from the Father, only-begotten, that is, from the substance of the Father, God from God, light from light, true God from true God, begotten not made, of one substance with the Father, through whom all things came into being, things in Heaven and things on Earth.'

In the same way, Jesus progressed from faithful Son to High Priest, we, too, have to start by learning to be faithful sons in our relationship with God. Jesus said, if you have seen Me, you have seen my Father, for the Father and I are one.

In the relationship between a spiritual father to a spiritual son, we need to show the true nature of God to the world. Jesus came to reveal God as a Father. Today, we need this same spirit of sonship that Jesus had with His Father. The Father loves the Son, and the Son loves the Father. The nature of God is Father, and God is love.

Jesus prayed in John 17:21 that the world needs to believe that the Father sent the Son. However, the Church needs to show the same unity in our relationships inside the Church for this to happen. The secret to winning nations is not necessarily better organisations, preaching, or even more churches. Love is the key, love that joins people's hearts together, the Church in unity. This will draw the world into the Church to find salvation.

In the fullness of time, Jesus was born a child in Bethlehem's manger. Though never relinquishing His divinity, though, without sin, Jesus became a man (Philippians 2:5–7). Being a man, He experienced the limitations of humanity, demonstrating for us a way of life under the government of God, always doing the will of the Father (Hebrews 10:9). In His humanity, the Scriptures tell us that **"So the child grew and became strong in spirit and was in the deserts till the day of his manifestation to Israel." Luke 1:80 (NKJV). Hebrews 5:8 (NKJV)** states: **"though He was a Son, yet He learned obedience by the**

things which He suffered." Yet if Jesus never sinned, how could He "learn obedience"?

As Jesus grew toward maturity, He, like all human children, was able to take on more and more responsibility. The older He became, the more demands His father and mother could place on Him in obedience, and the more complex the Heavenly Father's guidance became. With each increasingly difficult task, even when it involved some suffering (Hebrews 5:8), Jesus' human moral ability and His ability to obey under more difficult circumstances increased. Yet in all this, He never sinned (Hebrews 4:15).

The Father finally recognised Jesus openly when the heavens opened at His baptism. The Heavenly Father declared, **"And suddenly a voice came from heaven, saying, "This is My beloved Son, in whom I am well pleased." Matthews 3:17 (NKJV).** This signified Jesus' "adoption." It was now time for Jesus to begin His earthly ministry.

JOHN 5:19 (NKJV) "Then Jesus answered and said to them, 'Most assuredly, I say to you, the Son can do nothing of Himself, but what He sees the Father do; for whatever He does, the Son also does in like manner.'"

Jesus came into the world, sent by the Father.
He spoke the words of His Father to us.
He did the works of His Father.
He was crucified in obedience to the will of the Father.
He was raised again and ascended to the Father.
Jesus did not perform any ministry act until the pattern of Father to Son was fulfilled at the river Jordan.

The Lord Jesus, in whom God was manifested in the flesh, did not initiate His ministry until He was declared the Son of the Father.

As a Son, Jesus bore the exact "likeness" of the Father (John 14:9; II Corinthians 4:4; Hebrews 1:3). He did not seek His own glory, only the glory of His Father (John 8:50). He only wanted to do those things that pleased the Father. He was attentive to the Father's voice (John 8:28–29).

The Son was unwilling to allow death to stand in the way of Him and His Father's will. When He faced the prospect of a horrible death on the cross, He did not wish to inflict it upon Himself (Matthews 26:39). But He was willing to endure it to fulfil the Father's purpose and **"who for the joy that was set before Him endured the cross" Hebrews 12:2 (NKJV).** The Father's will was His overriding motivation. In all these things, Jesus was the "pattern" for us who desire to be sons of the Father.

The prodigal story became the display of three types of sons in the House of the Father.

Luke 15:11 (NKJV) "Then He said: "A certain man had two sons. And the younger of them said to his father, 'Father, give me the portion of goods that falls to me.' So, he divided to them his livelihood. And not many days after, the younger son gathered all together, journeyed to a far country, and there wasted his possessions with prodigal living. 14 But when he had spent all, there arose a severe famine in that land, and he began to be in want. Then he went and joined himself to a citizen of that country, and he sent him into his fields to feed swine. And he would gladly**

have filled his stomach with the pods that the swine ate, and no one gave him anything.

"But when he came to himself, he said, 'How many of my father's hired servants have bread enough and to spare, and I perish with hunger! I will arise and go to my father, and will say to him, "Father, I have sinned against heaven and before you, and I am no longer worthy to be called your son. Make me like one of your hired servants."'

"And he arose and came to his father. But when he was still a great way off, his father saw him and had compassion, and ran and fell on his neck and kissed him. 21 And the son said to him, 'Father, I have sinned against heaven and in your sight, and am no longer worthy to be called your son.'

"But the father said to his servants, 'Bring out the best robe and put it on him and put a ring on his hand and sandals on his feet. And bring the fatted calf here and kill it, and let us eat and be merry; for this, my son was dead and is alive again; he was lost and is found.' And they began to be merry.

"Now his older son was in the field. And as he came and drew near to the house, he heard music and dancing. So he called one of the servants and asked what these things meant. And he said to him, 'Your brother has come, and because he has received him safe and sound, your father has killed the fatted calf.'

"But he was angry and would not go in. Therefore, his father came out and pleaded with him. So he answered and said to his father, 'Lo, these many years I have been serving you; I never transgressed your commandment at any time; and yet you never gave me a young goat, that I might make merry with my friends. But as soon as this son of yours came, who has devoured your livelihood with harlots, you killed the fatted calf for him.'

"And he said to him, 'Son, you are always with me, and all that I have is yours."

The Father's perfect love restores us back to the original place of His presence:

The Father loved His son enough to let him leave home.

The Father loved His son so deeply that he watched every day, waiting for him to return home.

The Father loved his son so much that he did not condemn him for his wrong actions when he returned home. Instead, the Father forgave him and celebrated his return with a great feast!

Father's love activated the restoration of the "Prodigal" son, who became the restored son of inheritance.

We see the love of the Father inviting the older legalistic, jealous son to return to the House of the Father. This son represents the religious people living outside God's presence (House), criticising the feast and joy of celebrating God's real sons. Jesus refers to the Scribes, Pharisees, and Sadducees in this context. The same religious spirit is still very active today in the world and in the Church.

The Father's House represents the presence of God. "**In Your presence *is* fullness of joy; At Your right hand *are* pleasures forevermore.**" Psalms 16:11 (NKJV)

The things the Father gave the repented returning son represent the restoration of identity in the Father as a son of God: Living in His presence (House), living in a continuous feast, provision from the Provider God, authority as a son to a Father, ministry gifts were given and above all, forgiveness from the sin of the past.

John 14:1–4 (NKJV) "Let not your heart be troubled; you believe in God, believe also in Me. In My Father's house are many mansions; if it were not so, would I have told you. I go to prepare a place for you. And if I go and prepare a place for you, I will come again and receive you to Myself; that where I am, there you may be also. And where I go you know, and the way you know."

John explained that Jesus prepared a place for us on the cross! And then He will take us where He is, at the Father's right hand! In His presence. This promise is for now, for today. Not for one day, in the future!

The Father's love reached out to the rebellious prodigal son, who acted as an orphan slave. He abused the giftings of the Father, gave himself over to sin, to end up in an inferior (pig) lifestyle. Serving the pigs symbolises many backslidden rebellious sons creating their "own" ministries and trying to justify their low-grade lifestyles as the calling of God.

The Father's love reached out to the judgemental older son, who had access to the Father's House and presence but preferred to live far from the Father and detached from real love fellowship. He criticised the joyous life in the Father's House and was critical of the 'revival' movement of sinners returning to the Father. In the Church, these older brothers often become controlling leaders and pastors.

What and who is the way to Father?

JESUS ... One way! The only way!

John 14:5–11 (NKJV) "Thomas said to Him, 'Lord, we do not know where You are going, and how can we know the way?' Jesus said to him, 'I am the way, the truth, and the life. No one comes to the Father except through Me. If you had known Me, you would have known My Father also; and from now on you know Him and have seen Him.' Philip said to Him, 'Lord, show us the Father, and it is sufficient for us.' Jesus said to him, 'Have I been with you so long, and yet you have not known Me, Philip? He who has seen Me has seen the Father; so how can you say, 'Show us the Father'? Do you not believe that I am in the Father, and the Father in Me? The words that I speak to you I do not speak on My own authority; but the Father who dwells in Me does the works. Believe Me that I am in the Father and the Father in Me, or else believe Me for the sake of the works themselves.'"

We are not ignoring the price Jesus paid on the cross and agreeing with the world and liberal "Christians" who say there are many ways to God (the Father), of which Jesus is one of the ways! No, we are not deceived and confused! We know the truth and will keep on declaring it!

Receive the heart of the Father:

- Study the life of Jesus and His relationship with the Father. There are many scriptures in the New Testament in which we can learn about the unique relationship between Jesus and the Father

- Discover your position as a son of God; Galatians 4: From a child of God to a son of inheritance
- Be healed and transformed from your past father's wounds, pain and lies. This is a Romans 12:2 transformation of your mindset from a slave and an orphan spirit to your real identity as a son of God. Seek Godly anointed ministers or counsellors who can pray and minister to you.
- Remember that this is not an intellectual mind exercise! This is a Holy Spirit healing miracle!
- Develop your relationship with the Father as a son of God. Your spirit man calls out, "ABBA Father". Paul writes: **"For you did not receive the spirit of bondage again to fear, but you received the Spirit of adoption by whom we cry out, "Abba, Father"." Romans 8:15 (NKJV).**
- You need a spiritual heart transplant to receive the heart of the Father.
- Connect to a spiritual father if possible. Ask God to guide you in this process. Honour your leaders and your Church family while doing this.
- Don't only become a worthy son of God or even a trustworthy son to a spiritual father but also a Godly father to your family and a spiritual father to sons and daughters of God.

10. GOD WANTS TO ADOPT THE ORPHANS ON THIS ORPHAN PLANET

What is an orphan?

An orphan is someone without a father!
Our focus is to heal this orphan planet with healthy, Godly families and a fresh revelation of the character of God the Father!
We live on an orphan planet with millions of orphans!
God is calling us to heal the Orphan spirit with the Spirit of Adoption: the Spirit of the Father!

The truth is that satan was the first orphan, kicked out of Heaven because of his rebellion! He became Fatherless.

Adam & Eve became the second orphans kicked (eaten) out of Eden because of rebellion! They became orphans because they stopped living in the Father's presence and the Father's House. Because of them, all men & women are now orphans. We can say: Many Christians live as orphans because they don't know the Father's Spirit of adoption and sonship.

Many (most) Churches operate as orphanages, led by spiritual nurses with no spiritual fathers.

Some leaders try to be fathers but still operate in the mindset of an orphan (orphan spirit), so their sons will still be orphans as they have an 'orphan father'.

Africa is the continent of orphans. It was plundered for its fathers – its fathers were taken on ships across oceans.

Domestically, my home country South Africa was plundered with the homeland's separation philosophy. Thousands of fathers left home to work in cities, while their families had to be alone for months and years. Fathers went home to fight in a senseless war on the borders of our country.

The systems produced by the enemy brutalised the people and rendered them fatherless. Many leaders in our nation and Churches operate as orphans who, as mentioned above, produce orphans!!

The mission of Jesus was to return orphaned humanity to God and restore earthly family relationships to the way He intended them to be. Malachi prophesied that this would begin to happen when John the Baptist prepared the way for the Messiah: "He will turn the hearts of the fathers to their children, and the hearts of the children to their fathers; or else I will come and strike the land with a curse" (Malachi 4:6).

We, as ministers, need to understand that the orphan spirit can't only be cast out! Neither can it be taught out! It can only be healed out by real fathers who have the Spirit of the Father!!! Orphans must be adopted into the House and heart of the Father!! Adoption is the Biblical process of entering into the Kingdom of the Father!

Adoption into the Household (Church) of God must be taught, and healing must be facilitated by ministers who operate with the heart and anointing of the Father! Adoption means to be "son placed", not "son made". You are made a Son (child of God) when God's grace saves you. And, as a son, there are certain privileges and benefits that God, by His sovereign acts, has provided for those who are saved. No one gets son placed until they are presented as mature.

Creation and man were created to represent the nature and character of God. Adam was the son of God. The fall of man in the book of Genesis has resulted in the separation between man and his Father. When you lose your father, you suffer an unimaginable loss.

If you are a father, you may still operate in the culture of an orphan, and your sons will still be orphans even though they have you as a father. The orphan loses his father as well as his inheritance.

Losses associated with the culture of the orphan: E.g. the man came to be at enmity with his wife. Instead of addressing her as "bone of my bone and flesh of my flesh" (before the sin), he now, after he sins, refers to her as "the woman that you gave me" – no longer "flesh of my flesh". Before the fall, they were in perfect unity - inseparable. Man did not see the woman as a separate entity apart from himself. In **Ephesians 5:26–27 (A summary of the two verses) "he washes her with water that he might present her to himself ..."** She submits to his rule because his rule typifies the very nature of Christ. The mission of a man and a woman is to show the reunion between God and man based on the template of Christ and the Church.

Why did Cain murder Abel? He acted like an orphan. The culture of the orphan was first manifested in Genesis 4 when we see brother go against brother in a murderous frenzy.

The Spirit of adoption

Rom 8:14–15 "For as many as are led by the Spirit of God; they are the <u>sons</u> (Huios) <u>of God</u>. For you have not received the spirit of bondage again to fear, but you have received the <u>Spirit of adoption</u> (to sons) by which we cry, Abba, Father!"

Rom 8:23. "And not only they but ourselves also, which have the first fruits of the Spirit, even we ourselves groan within ourselves, waiting for the Adoption, to wit, the redemption of our body."

Galatians 4:5 "To redeem them that were under the law, that we might receive the adoption of sons."

He delivers & heals you from your orphan spirit through the spirit of adoption! Let Jesus heals you entirely from all your father wounds.

The Son receives His identity from the Father, and the Son reveals the Father.

With adoption, the son gets recognised as one who could faithfully represent the father. He has arrived at the point of maturity where the father can entrust him with overseeing the family business. The son becomes the "heir" of his father's inheritance. Birth gives one the right to the inheritance, but adoption gives one participation in the inheritance.

As your spiritual father, I cannot fulfil the place of your biological father; As your spiritual father, I am not the father of your spirit; God is! But I will do my best to reveal to you the Father's heart and help you receive healing and the spirit of adoption into sonship.

I have fathered my sons and other people's sons and daughters, and some became real sons & fathers. Others are still prodigal sons living with the pigs. Others are still like the older brother, living outside the House of the Father.

The following scripture represents the complete process of becoming children of God, who again become the sons of God. Who now are the sons of inheritance, who know Father as Daddy, ABBA.

Gal 4:1–7 (NKJV) "Now I say that the heir, as long as he is a child, does not differ at all from a slave, though he is master of all, but is under guardians and stewards until the time appointed by the father. Even so we, when we were children, were in bondage under the elements of the world. But when the fullness of the time had come, God sent forth His Son, born of a woman, born under the law, to redeem those who were under the law, that we might receive the <u>adoption as sons</u>. And because you are sons, God has sent forth the Spirit of His Son into your hearts, crying out, "Abba, Father!" Therefore, you are no longer a slave but a son, and if a son, then you are an heir of God through Christ.

The most important aspect of your maturity is your intimate connection with ABBA Father. You can, and you should know Him as your Daddy. You should often have encounters with ABBA Father. You must get to know His voice. You must know and experience the reality of being a son of the Father. Your connection to a healthy real spiritual father will accelerate your growth, influence and anointing.

11. CHARACTERISTICS OF FATHERLESS CHILDREN AND ADULTS

Hundreds of research statistics regarding the effects of an absent father on sons and daughters are available. Most of them come to similar conclusions. I will draw from them to give a general summary of the shocking facts we face today.

There is a shortage of fathers in today's world and in the Church. The emotional and spiritual effects of this have been nothing less than catastrophic! The following are some of the symptoms of fatherlessness which can be applied to both natural and spiritual fathers.

The National Fatherhood Initiative[1] in the USA compiles information from various sources on the effects of fatherlessness on many social problems, including poverty, maternal and child health, imprisonment, crime, teen pregnancy, child abuse, drug and alcohol abuse, education, and childhood obesity. Here are some of the disturbing data they have collected:

- Children in father-absent homes are five times more likely to be poor.
- Infant mortality rates are 1.8 times higher for infants of unmarried mothers than married mothers.

64

- Youths in absent-father households have significantly higher odds of imprisonment than those in mother-father families.
- Youths are far more at risk of first substance abuse without a highly involved father.
- Being raised by a single mother increases the risk of teen pregnancy.
- Fatherless children are twice as likely to drop out of school.
- Compared to living with both parents, living in a single-parent home doubles the risk that a child will suffer physical, emotional, or educational neglect.
- An absent father can affect a person's economic prospects beyond childhood.

Consequences that result from the absence of a loving father:

- **Lack of Identity.**

The father is responsible for providing or establishing the identity of everyone who comes from him. The father establishes the individual's identity. Natural and spiritual children who grow up without fathers are insecure and unaware of their identity as individuals or as sons and daughters of God.

- **Sons who do not know how to be sons and good fathers.**

For a man to become a good father and practice his role and responsibility as a father, he first needs to learn from a good role model, one who is visible, easy to imitate, and easy to learn from. Men who never experienced a father's love do not know how to behave like fathers. Men will not have the knowledge and guidance to understand their fatherly responsibilities unless God intervenes.

- **The absence of a loving father affects our relationship with the Heavenly Father.**

The inability to establish a relationship with the Father has nothing to do with God; instead, it results from one's own negative experiences with one's natural father. Abuse, cruelty, maltreatment, rejection, lack of love and protection, carelessness and abandonment prevent people from establishing a healthy relationship with their Heavenly Father.

- **The absence of a loving father causes society to become violent.**

Juvenile delinquency increased as divorce became an accepted practice in society. Divorce led to a breakdown in family values and the destruction of the values that allow people to have better and improved relationships.

- **The absence of a loving father can cause a curse to fall upon the family.**

Simply being able to procreate does not automatically make men fathers. Being a father is a godly task entrusted to men by the Father. A man's success is measured by how good a father he is with his family, Church, and disciples, not by his diplomas, wealth, or fame. A man is also said to be a good father if he does an excellent job in the role God has entrusted him to, that of a father in His Kingdom.

Some of the effects of fathers' absence on their daughter

- Teenage pregnancy
- Sexual identity disorder. Sexual dysfunctional.
- Traumatised emotions
- Financial disorder and poverty.
- Educational slow development.
- Low self-esteem.
- Fear of intimacy.

The primary source or root of nearly every problem humanity faces (with girls and women) is the absence of a father.

- **The effect of a poor father-daughter relationship**

The relationship between a daughter and her father is a significant factor in the growth and development of a female. If a girl's father was absent, negligent or abusive during her childhood, the negative effects of that relationship could severely damage her identity, especially her sexual identity. Beyond modelling behaviour that his daughter will expect from other men in her life, the interaction between a father and his daughter will help form her identity and what she views as normal roles for a man and a woman.

- **Early Sexual Development**

The quality of the father-daughter relationship can affect the timing of sexual development in girls. The experience of an absent or emotionally distant father can become evident in the onset of menstruation and body hair growth at an earlier age, reveals psychologist Lynda G. Boothroyd, PhD, in her book

"Father Absence. Parent-Daughter Relationships and Partner Preferences." These daughters are also more likely to have sexual intercourse earlier than their counterparts with better father-daughter relationships.

- **Poor Intimate Relationships**

According to the research of Lynda Boothroyd, women who have poor relationships with their fathers are more likely to choose mates whose personalities and characteristics differ widely from that of their fathers. They were found to prefer romantic partners who had less masculine features. These women were also more likely to experience marital difficulty later in life or be sexually promiscuous.

- **Poor Communication**

Linda Nielsen, PhD, author of the book "Between Fathers and Daughters: Enriching or Rebuilding Your Adult Relationship," states that a poor father-daughter relationship significantly affects how a female communicates and relates to others, especially men. If there is poor communication between father and daughter, she will likely have communication problems with other men.

- **Trust Issues**

When a father is absent, whether physically or emotionally, from his daughter's life, especially during childhood, it may seriously affect the daughter's ability to form a strong bond with not only him, but it may have a "trickle-down" effect on all the other men who will come into her life. She may find it difficult to open up to other men and even to her own father for fear that she will be abandoned or disappointed again.

In a healthy father-daughter relationship, a daughter feels nurtured by her father and acknowledged as on her way to becoming a woman. Like a son, a daughter needs to experience the presence and love of a stable father growing up.

The Effects of an Absent Father on an Infant Son's Development

The US Census Bureau records (2012) that one in every three children, amounting to 24 million in America, live in homes without their biological fathers. Reasons for absent fathers vary from voluntary abandonment, military service, and divorce to death. The absence of a father affects a male infant's emotional, cognitive and social development throughout his life.

Bonding helps stimulate an infant's cognitive and social development; it begins during pregnancy. If the father was present during this period, the infant learns to recognise his voice. After birth, parents establish bonding by touching, talking, answering cries and making eye contact with the baby. Infants with affectionate fathers form more secure attachments than those without fathers. An innate connection with the father helps prepare the infant for interactions with other males. If the baby does not develop this connection, it becomes hard for him to get used to other males later in life.

The presence of a responsive and attentive father in an infant's life creates a sense of security. The infant feels confident enough to explore his surroundings with the knowledge of a father who responds quickly to his cries. These infants are emotionally secure and develop better social connections with their peers as they grow older. In most instances, an absent father results in delayed social and emotional development for the child.

The presence of a father in an infant's life helps the child learn how to deal with trauma and aggression as the masculine self develops. Male children without fathers tend to experience nightmares about terror and violence. Therefore, infants with absent fathers tend to exhibit aggressive behaviours and are more prone to get into trouble at school later in life.

More Statistics in the USA. (Statistics in the 1st world countries are very similar to the USA, and in the 3rd world countries, even worse.

- 63 per cent of youth suicides are from fatherless homes (Source: US DHHS, Bureau of the Census)
- 90 per cent of all homeless and runaway children are from fatherless homes
- 85 per cent of all children that exhibit behavioural disorders come from fatherless homes (Source: Center for Disease Control)
- 80 per cent of rapists motivated by displaced anger come from fatherless homes (Source: Criminal Justice & Behavior, Vol 14, p. 403–26, 1978.)
- 71per cent of all high school dropouts come from fatherless homes (Source: National Principals Association Report on the State of High Schools.)
- 75 per cent of all adolescent patients in chemical abuse centres come from fatherless homes (Source: Rainbows for all God`s Children.)
- 70 per cent of juveniles in state-operated institutions come from fatherless homes (Source: US Dept. of Justice, Special Report, Sept 1988)
- 85 per cent of all youths sitting in prisons grew up in a fatherless home (Source: Fulton Co. Georgia jail populations, Texas Dept. of Corrections 1992)

- Children living in two-parent households with a poor relationship with their fathers are 68 per cent more likely to smoke, drink, or use drugs than children in healthy two-parent households.
- Children with fathers who are involved are forty per cent less likely to repeat a grade in school.
- Adolescent girls raised in two-parent homes with involved fathers are significantly less likely to be sexually active than girls raised without involved fathers.

These statistics point to an epidemic rather than just a problem and cannot be ignored. No group of people is immune to the effects.

Men without fathers.

Growing up without a father figure profoundly affects boys and lasts into manhood. Boys need a father figure to learn how to be a man. Without this influence in their lives, boys are at risk of growing into men who end up displaying behavioural and emotional problems.I

Low Self-Esteem

In his MentalHealth.com article "The Politics of Divorce: When Children Become Pawns, " psychologist Alan Schwartz writes that when a parent is absent, "children may blame themselves, believing something is wrong with them. They believe that they must not be deserving or lovable. Children also develop the belief that the absent parent is bad, and so, through genetics, they must also be bad. Children of divorce, where one parent has sole custody, grow up to have significantly lower self-esteem than children of parents who have joint custody or whose parents remain married. This is especially true in men, who learn to be men mostly through their interactions with a father figure. Without those interactions, men can grow up unsure of how they should behave as husbands and fathers."

Some men continually face insecurities that negatively impact their business, ministry, and marriage relationships. They never fully trust their abilities, so they don't always trust others around them to do the right thing. This sense of inferiority causes them to try to hide their low self-esteem by projecting a personality full of confidence, but inside their souls, they are always afraid.

Negative Behaviour

Adolescent boys look to their father figures to tell them if they are good enough to be men, writes psychologist Frank Pittman in an article for Psychology Today entitled "Fathers and Sons." Adolescent boys experience emotional pain without paternal approval, leading to attempts to prove themselves. These include intense competition with other boys, engaging in risky behaviours, and criminal "tough guy" behaviour intended to scare the world into seeing them as men. Psychologist Marie Hartwell-Walker reinforces this in her PsychCentral.com article "Daddies Do Make a Difference." She reports that men who grow up without fathers are more likely to abuse alcohol and drugs and to get into trouble with law enforcement.

Difficulties Bonding

Hartwell-Walker writes that men who grow up without a father figure also have more problems bonding with their own children. Having never experienced a father-son bond, they are unsure how to develop that relationship with their children. Men who had absent fathers are more likely to be absent fathers themselves. These men were also never taught how to have healthy relationships with women and tend to have higher break-up and divorce rates than men who grow up with a father's influence.

Emotional Distress

Boys who grow up without a father show higher stress levels to daily challenges – traffic or dealing with a boss, for example, writes Kathleen Doheny in her PsychCentral.com article, "Good Dad, Good Coping Skills Later," A boy's relationship with his mother also helps to reduce his stress levels as an adult. Still, the effect is smaller than that of a father. A good relationship with his father teaches a son to solve problems better, allowing him, as a man, to deal with everyday stress in more valuable ways. According to Schwartz, men who grow up without paternal influence are more likely to experience depression and anxiety.

Incredible competitive drive due to comparisons with other men

Some men's insecurities result in them constantly comparing themselves with other men. If they are ministers, they compare themselves with fellow ministers in their region. They always try to outdo other men as if ministry were a sport. For example, I know some ministers who, when talking about themselves or their ministries, constantly make statements like "our Church is growing in record numbers," or "We have the largest pastoral group in the city", or "We are the Church called of God to reach the city." They use competitive language with a super-spiritual religious tinge, but it is a merely fleshly competition that is not purely motivated by the leading of the Lord.

There is strong independence because of a lack of trust in all authority figures.

Some men who have experienced fatherlessness have difficulty inwardly submitting to any form of spiritual authority, even if they outwardly attempt to do so. They mostly make their own decisions without getting accurate counsel. If they get counsel, they will ultimately do what they want anyway because they don't believe anyone looks out for their interests entirely.

They have a selfish ambition driven by an internal desire to please their fathers.

Many fatherless men are psychologically living their lives to prove to their fathers (whether alive or dead) that they are valuable and worthy of their father's love (this can also apply to spiritual fathers). Interestingly, they may even hate their fathers emotionally but not be aware that they are emotionally geared to secure their fathers' approval finally.

There is an inability to relate to their own biological and spiritual sons.

Many men do not emotionally connect with their sons and daughters.

One man I know didn't do anything but play video games with his son. When I asked why he couldn't have a decent conversation with his son, he said he tried but didn't know how. He confessed that he had no idea how to be a father to his son because he had never had a father.

They cannot relate to a genuine spiritual father due to a lack of comfort around spiritual fathers.

Many fatherless men with anger and trust issues regarding their fathers have a hard time with those in the Body of Christ called to be spiritual fathers, especially ones assigned to that man. They get nervous and try hard to know how to relate to and please them. Or they hide their struggles because they fear the spiritual father will use them against them and hold them back from their destiny.

There is confusion as to their purpose and identity in Christ.

Many fatherless men have difficulty figuring out who they are and what they are called to do. They struggle with their identity. They may even be the most successful businesspeople in the world, but they are never sure of themselves, often grapple with confusion, fear, and anger, and don't understand the root cause. Some of the highest suicide rates in the world are in the most affluent demographics of our nation. This shows that worldly or even ministerial success can never fill the vast void in the souls of many fatherless men.

When a man feels threatened by the success of his spiritual sons (example of the prodigal son's older brother).

When fatherless men become spiritual leaders, some tend to use spiritual sons to advance their own agendas but never make room for them to blossom and reach their potential in Christ. They feel threatened when their sons begin to mature; they are afraid to let them preach or lead at their highest capacity. They do this because the insecurities in their souls cause them to compare themselves to their sons. This torments them, ultimately causing them to hold their sons under their thumbs. Consequently, many sons become frustrated and rebellious, start their own Churches, or leave the faith.

For many men, it is hard to connect to the love of God the Father.

Some fatherless men have a hard time fellowshipping and enjoying their Father in Heaven, as they have a works mentality and try to approach Him with their own sense of perfection to prove their worth. This is because they didn't have a good earthly model of fatherhood from their natural fathers and did not understand how to relate to God the Father and His unconditional love.

Having an autocratic style of leadership in Churches, businesses and families

Because fatherless men are never emotionally connected with their earthly fathers, many do not know how to relate or trust others who work for them or are under their care in their families. They may even preach teamwork, but ultimately, the decision-making process is limited to what they want. The result is a top-down autocratic style of leadership that doesn't leave room for meaningful input, counsel, or shared leadership decisions.

There are often feelings of loneliness and emptiness, for nothing satisfies the hole in their hearts.

No matter how many people are around them, many fatherless men often feel like outsiders, never able to fully enjoy the company of others as they are uncomfortable in their own skin. They don't know where they fit in and are constantly gripped with a sense of emptiness that no amount of activity, crowds, money, accolades, or success could fill.

There is an inability to enjoy the present and a desire to always focus on an unreachable future.

Many fatherless men are constantly striving, never satisfied, and never happy. Thus, they always look to a better future and never enjoy the present. We often put our own spin on events in our lives and project wrong motives onto others because we ourselves have impure motives. At best, many fatherless leaders have superficial relationships with those they deem threats to their leadership. They keep them at arm's length unless they need them for something that advances their agendas.

[1] https://www.fatherhood.org/father_factor.asp, February 6, 2008.

12. KNOWING THE FATHER'S VOICE

God formed man out of clay from the dust of the ground, and He inserted into this form a spirit which came out of the very person of God. Thus God is the father of our spirits. When God imparted His Spirit into man out of His own person, He created a being compatible with God's nature. Is it not amazing to think that God designed us so that we could communicate with Him? Making man unique among all created beings? The problem came with the fall of man when man lost his ability to hear God. So man's spirit became insensitive to the voice of God. From that time on, man's own voice would constantly compete with the voice of God.

"The greatest example of knowing the voice of God is recorded in **John 5:19–20 (NKJV): "Truly, truly, I say to you, the Son can do nothing of Himself unless it is something He sees the Father doing; for whatever the Father does, these things the Son also does in like manner."** To follow this example, we must learn that prayer is vital to hearing His voice, but there comes a time when we must still listen. For the Father loves the Son and shows Him all things He Himself is doing; first, we must see others applying what they hear from the Father; then, we must begin to follow that example.

The voice of God is the essence of life! It can be amplified and confirmed by a spiritual father to a son. I find my life, way, words, answers, and directions in the voice of God. It all comes from my Father to me, His son.

In the Old Testament, the usual way of hearing God's voice was through the prophets. But in the New Covenant, God speaks to and through His sons.

Most Christians and Church systems operate mainly with the old order of Preacher to the crowd, Priest to the tribe, and Pastor to the congregation. God's new system in these last days is Father to son. Mature sons (fathers) to sons.

Hebrews 1:1–3 (NKJV) "God, who at various times and in various ways spoke in time past to the fathers by the prophets, has in these last days spoken to us by His Son, whom He has appointed heir of all things, through whom also He made the worlds."

When we study the difference between Old Testament prophetic ministry and the prophets of the New Covenant, we need to understand that there are significant differences, which we will not expand on now. As we saw in the New Testament, the role of prophets has changed compared to the Old Testament, but they are still essential to the Church and are seen as vital to the foundation of the Church together with New Covenant Apostles (fathers)

What is very important is that God's Fatherly voice is released to sons, and God the Father loves to use mature sons (who we call fathers) to confirm and clarify the Father's voice.

Adam and Eve walked with the Father in the garden (His presence), and His voice was constantly present. After they sinned, they lost the voice of the Father.

John 6:63 (NKJV) " It is the Spirit who gives life; the flesh profits nothing. <u>The words that I speak to you are spirit, and they are life</u>."

As sons of our ABBA Father, we have the privilege of hearing His voice constantly. The atmosphere of His presence is filled with Spirit Words that give us life.

2 Cor 3:6 (NKJV) " (God) who also made us sufficient as ministers of the new covenant, not of the letter but of the Spirit; for the letter kills, but the Spirit gives life.**

For those who ask: Isn't the Bible the Word of God, and is it not enough just to read it? We deeply love the Bible, and the Spirit of God can and will speak many revelational Words through the written Word, which becomes life to us through the Spirit of God. But be aware that in our religious world, many people worship the Book (the letter) and not the God of the Book. They esteem the Book of the Bible higher than the presence of God. People who are not living in and from the presence of God will not understand this statement: God speaks out of His presence, and the Bible confirms what we hear in the presence. The presence of God must be the focus of every meeting and worship service. It must be the focus of our lives. The presence releases the voice! God is a talking God who loves to speak to His sons and daughters all the time!

ABBA Father speaks to sons from His presence, and the voice of God can and must, be amplified by His sons and daughter to this world!

13. LIVING FROM THE THIRD ROOM OF THE TABERNACLE: THE MOST HOLY PLACE, THE PLACE OF THE FATHER

This chapter is partly an extract from my book "Unlocking the Third Reformation." I use the Tabernacle's hidden message to explain the New Testament gospel. The focus is primarily on Jesus, who represents the First Room of the Tabernacle, and how He is taking us to the Third Room, the room and place of the Father.

My book about the Third Reformation focuses on the following:

- Celebrating 500 years after the first Reformation, which started with Martin Luther, Calvin, and many other reformists.
- The Second Reformation was the Holy Spirit outpouring which started the Pentecostal movement in early 1900.
- A new Reformation? The re-formation of a de-formed Church with weak-formed members, living an un-formed powerless lifestyle.
- Why do we need a new, fresh, third reformation? This is what the book is about!

I use the image and allegory of the three-room Tabernacle of Moses, the temple of God, and the earthly manifestation of the presence of God, to explain the unique New Testament three-fold process of personal and Church life reformation into Christ.

The Tabernacle model is a foundation for our three-fold Reformation journey to mature in Christ and be positioned with the Father.

The present revival of God worldwide symbolises the beginning of the third wave or third Reformation since the first coming of Jesus. Everything happens to prepare the Church and her people for the final return of Jesus Christ.

Celebrating: **1ˢᵗ Reformation 500 years ago!**
                         2ⁿᵈ Reformation, 100 years ago!
                         3ʳᵈ Reformation, Now presently

Hebrews 8:5 (NKJV)" who serve <u>the copy and shadow of the heavenly things</u>, as Moses was divinely instructed when he was about to make the Tabernacle. For He said, "See that you make all things according to the pattern shown you on the mountain."

Rev 11:19 (NKJV) "Then God's <u>temple in heaven</u> was opened, and within his temple was seen the <u>ark of his covenant</u>."

- Jesus is the Tabernacle.
- Jesus fulfilled every aspect of the Tabernacle.
- Because of Jesus, we can now become the Tabernacle, the temple of God. (1 Corinthians 3:16–17).
- Jesus's ultimate purpose in fulfilling His journey to earth, from being a baby to the Cross and the resurrection

(also fulfilling the journey through the Tabernacle), is to reveal the Father and take us to the Father.

- The Third Room, the Most Holy Place, is the Place of the Father, the place where Jesus is seated at the right hand of the Father, the place from where we can do the same works as Jesus and even greater works (John 14:12), and ask anything in Jesus Name, and the Father will answer it. **John 14:13-14 (NKJV), "And whatever you ask in My name, that I will do, that the Father may be glorified in the Son. If you ask anything in My name, I will do it."**

- The Tabernacle is **not** only a description of our journey of going to Heaven, but it is a demonstration of our intended living and ruling in this life and our life to come, being seated with Jesus at the Father's right hand.

Jesus is the Tabernacle of God and fulfilled every requirement to be seated at the place of the Father:

The Tabernacle is the best description and display of a person becoming a 'new creation' and being 'born again'. The first step is taken by entering through the door – Jesus is the door – but the aim is to eventually enter into the Third Room, the place of the Father – the Most Holy Place.

The Tabernacle model can be a step-by-step guide to teach new disciples their journey to maturity. This model is also an excellent tool to use as a framework to counsel an individual in incredible detail. In my experience, I have found it to be the best model for Church leaders to use as a foundation for growth and the type of culture needed to develop within a healthy, growing Church. It teaches one how to progressively go deeper, to worship fully in spirit and truth.

When Jesus died on the Cross, there was an earthquake, graves were opened, and the veil (curtain) to the Most Holy Place was torn from top to bottom. Permanent access to God's presence was established. We now have an open-plan tabernacle. The Ark of the Covenant is accessible to all believers because we are all Kings and Priests *now*. **1 Peter 2:9 (NKJV); "But you *are* a chosen generation, a royal priesthood, a holy nation, His own special people, that you may proclaim the praises of Him who called you out of darkness into His marvellous light."**

Jesus said the same about an open Heaven. Jesus invited us into His presence at the right hand of the Father. The open Heaven is represented by the torn veil that is still open now! **Revelation 4:1–2 (NKJV); "After these things I looked, and behold, a door *standing* open in heaven. And the first voice which I heard *was* like a trumpet speaking with me, saying, "Come up here, and I will show you things which must take place after this. And immediately I was in the spirit, and behold, a throne was set in heaven, and one sat on the throne."**

The Third Room, the Most Holy Place, is where the heavenly presence of God is manifest, which we can access and enjoy in this life and the life to come.

We now have access, and it is part of our destiny, our inheritance, to sit with Jesus at the Father's right hand! **Ephesians 2:4–6 (NKJV), "But God, who is rich in mercy, because of His great love with which He loved us, even when we were dead in trespasses, made us alive together with Christ (by grace you have been saved), and raised us up together, and <u>made us sit together in the heavenly places</u> in Christ Jesus".**

Revelation 3:21 (NKJV), "To him who overcomes I will grant to <u>sit with Me on My throne</u>, as I also overcame and sat down with My Father on His throne."

It is evident that we are invited to sit with Jesus at the Father's right hand. That's our place with the Father. That is the position from where we pray, heal and preach. That's where we'll hear Father's voice very personally and very clearly. It's the place of joy, peace and love. It was also the place where the Prodigal son was seated at the Father's feast at their home. The Prodigal son was cleansed (First Room). He received a ring of authority, a new dress of righteousness, new shoes of sonship (slaves went bare feet), and a fatted calf (abundant provision). He received a 'more than enough' provision, and then he was invited into the Father's house to celebrate and party with the whole household. This is an ultimate expression of the Third Room, the Most Holy Place, the Place of the Father. The older brother was standing (and living) on the outside, outside of the Third Room, outside the place of joy, away from the presence of the Father. The older brother represents the many religious and traditional people constantly criticising the new moves of the Spirit. Read Luke 15:11 again and ask yourself whether you are a prodigal in the pig's pen or the prodigal who came to his mind and surrendered himself to be a full son of the Father; or are you an older brother who is sceptical and critical about those who party with the Father?

**You are seated with Jesus Christ
at the right hand of the Father...
The Place of the Father,
The Father's House!**

Every Christian can and should live in the presence of God's glory in the Most Holy Place! We may boldly enter and live in God's Holy presence because of the Blood of the

Lamb. **Hebrews 10:19 (NKJV); "Therefore, brethren, having boldness to enter the Holiest by the blood of Jesus,".**

You can enter into and live from the Most Holy Place. This becomes your place of worship, your home, your place of rulership with Jesus, at the Father's right hand.

Hundreds of years before Jesus, King David created a prophetic picture of what the eternal Tabernacle (temple) would one day look like by erecting a tent in Jerusalem with open sides; the Ark of the Covenant in the middle, open, for all, to see, and people could dance and celebrate all around it inside the tent. It was "an open plan presence of God" without the First and Second Room. For a moment, King David created a prophetic picture of what would happen after the Cross of Jesus. In the New Testament, in Acts 15:16, James refers to the prophecy in **Amos. 9:11 (NKJV), "After this, I will return, and will rebuild the tabernacle of David, which has fallen down; I will rebuild its ruins, and I will set it up".** This confirms that in the same way, David gave open access to the Most Holy Place, we can now experience access to God with similar freedom. All believers can now worship and live in the presence of the Ark of the Covenant, where the presence of the Father is personally manifested. This is probably why David was called 'the man after God's own heart!'

Acts 13:22 (NKJV) says, "And when He had removed him, He raised up for them David as king, to whom also He gave testimony and said, 'I have found David, the son of Jesse, a man after My own heart, who will do all My will.'"

A question to you: Do you see yourself as a King-Priest who has the right to enter boldly into Father's holy presence?

Can you see yourself under the covering of the Blood of Jesus, which gives you the right not only to come into the presence of God but also to sit with Jesus at the right hand of the Father?

God is a Trinity being, and so is everything He is doing. The following table is a simple explanation of the miracle of God, who operates nearly everything in three aspects. The Outer Court (First Room) displays what Jesus came to do for us. The Holy Place (Second Room) displays the Holy Spirit's work. The Third Room is our study's focus, displaying the miracle of our unity with ABBA Father.

Many topics in the Bible are revealed in a three-fold mystery:

Outer Court	Holy Place	Most Holy Place
Jesus	Holy Spirit	Father
Feast of Passover	Feast of Pentecost	Feast of Tabernacles
Ps 100> Thanksgiving	Praise	Worship
Psalms	Hymns	Spiritual Songs
Jesus Christ (Saviour)	Christ Jesus (The Anointed One)	The LORD (Christ in us)
Way	Truth	Life
Born Again	Spirit Filled	Maturity (Full of the Spirit)
Mat 28:19> Baptism in Water (Jesus)	Baptism in the Spirit	Baptism in Father
Priest	Prophet	King
Levite	Priest	High Priest
Out of Egypt	Wilderness	Promised Land (Canaan)
Justification	Sanctification	Glorification
Offering	Tithe	First fruit
Ark of Covenant: Manna = Grace	2 Tables: God's Principles (God's WORD on how to love)	Aaron's blossoming Rod: Godly Anointed Leadership
1 Cor 13:13. Faith	Hope	Love
Rom 12:2 > Good will	Acceptable will	Perfect will
Milk	Bread	Meat
1 John 2:13 > Little Children	Young Men	Fathers
Body	Soul	Spirit
Gal 4:1-7. 'Nėpios' Babies	'Teknon' Children	'Huios' Sons of inheritance
1 John 5:6-8. Three who witness in Heaven: The Word (Jesus)	The Holy Spirit	The Father
1 John 5:6-8. Three who witness on earth: The Blood	The Water	The Spirit

The Altar of Incense started in the Second Room but moved into the Most Holy Place in the New Testament because of the torn veil.

Hebrews 9:3–5 (NKJV), "and behind the second veil, the part of the Tabernacle which is called the Holiest of All, which had the <u>golden censer</u> and the ark of the covenant overlaid on all sides with gold, in which *were* the golden pot that had the manna, Aaron's rod that budded, and the tablets of the covenant; and above it were the cherubim of glory overshadowing the mercy seat. Of these things, we cannot now speak in detail."

The golden Altar of Incense represents worship and prayers. The prescribed incenses used were a mixture of spices and salt (Exodus 30:34–35), and they were burned to create an aroma in the Ark's presence, representing God's presence. It's important to understand that the literal tabernacle worship in the Old Testament was a type that is fulfilled in the spiritual worship in the New Testament. We now worship in the Spirit and pray in the Spirit in the New Testament. Jesus told the Samaritan woman that Father is looking for worshippers who are worshipping Him in Spirit and Truth (John 4:23–24). This was made possible by the Cross for Spirit-filled believers. This is also the reason why the Altar of Incense has moved from the Second Room into the Third Room, the Most Holy Place. Believers that understand this principle quickly move from singing soulish songs in an Old Testament style to a New Testament style, engaging with Holy Spirit in their worship.

There has been a strong spirit of intercession and worship movement worldwide in the last couple of years. It is based on the prophetic call for harp and bowl intercession and worship as we find it in **Revelation 5:8 (NKJV)**, which describes the twenty-four elders, each "had a **harp**" and "were holding golden

bowls full of incense, which are the prayers of the saints." Therefore, it refers to us and, most probably, to God's prophetic people engaging in prophetic worship.

This is a clear call from heaven that we take our rightful place as Holy Spirit worshippers and worship Father and Jesus continuously as the primary activity of the people of God. Church services should focus primarily on Spirit worship in and from the presence of God. Revival Churches spontaneously spend lengthy sessions just worshipping God in the Spirit.

My question to you is, what kind of worship are you offering to God? Are you only singing a few soul songs or offering Holy Spirit-led worship? Do you experience the presence of God in your worship? Are you part of a Church family that knows how to worship in the Spirit and intimately with God in His presence, a Church that honours God's presence more than a program?

The main piece of furniture in the Most Holy Place was the Ark of the Covenant, an Acacia wooden box covered with pure gold. Over the box were two angels (Cherubs), overshadowing the solid gold cover called the Mercy Seat. Inside the Ark were the three articles on-demand from God: The Golden Bowl filled with manna, the two Tablets of the Law, and the Rod of Aaron, which sprouted, budded, blossomed, and produced ripe almonds! (Numbers 17:8).

What is the message the Ark conveys to us?

First, we must understand that this Third Room is the Place of the Father. Jesus went to prepare a place for us at the Father's right hand, with Him! Remember that Jesus said in **John 14:6 (NKJV), "No one can come to the Father, except through Me!"** Before that, He had said: **"I am the way, the**

truth, and the life", the three doors to the Most Holy Place. Jesus leads us to the Father. Your ultimate goal is to meet the Father, to live in and from His presence while ministering His MERCY and GOODNESS to the world. In Christ, **you must become what the Ark of the Covenant represents;** the Mercy seat, the carrier of the three articles inside the Ark. The ark was built from Acacia wood, representing your flesh, covered with gold; the presence and glory of God, served by the Cherubim (Angels; who are ministering beings serving us, Hebrews 1:14). The three articles inside the Ark represent unique encounters and principles God taught His people. Jesus fulfilled the symbolism and the meaning of the Ark and its contents, and in Him, we should now be the carriers and manifestation of the Ark as well.

The MANNA is the representation of the GOODNESS and GRACE of God. We receive it because God is good and not because we have done anything good! The goodness of God is the main message of the Bible! Manna represents the Word in season at this time. We should become the carriers of the goodness of God. You must be a 'goodness' preacher and manifest God's goodness and grace.

God personally gave the two **TABLETS OF THE LAW** to His people to teach them how to love! How to love God is reflected in the first Tablet and is described in the first four laws or principles. How to love our neighbours is reflected in the Second Tablet containing the last six principles of the Law. God is writing His laws into your heart and giving you the ability to love unconditionally with the power and love of the Holy Spirit (Romans 5:5). LOVE must manifest in your life. You must walk in love, demonstrate love, and love God by being a passionate lover and worshipper of God.

The STAFF or ROD of Aaron represents Godly anointed leadership, those you are accountable to and aligned with. The rod was placed in the Ark because leaders rebelled against Moses. God killed the rebels and said that the rod should be a reminder of the necessity for God's people to align themselves with God's chosen leaders, those whom He has anointed to lead God's people.

These three articles inside the Ark must characterise your lifestyle and commitment as you serve God the Father. They must be written in your heart and reflect your character.

Are you becoming an anointed leader and father whom God can trust to lead His people? Are you committed to your divinely appointed leadership and honouring them? Are you connected with and aligned with Godly leadership who can act as spiritual fathers or mentors in your life?

The Mercy seat symbolises the place where the High Priest met God when he came into the Most Holy Place once a year to intercede and atone for God's people. Jesus is the eternal High Priest who paid for our sins once and for all by His Blood, enabling us to live in the mercy and goodness of God daily and forever. Jesus fulfilled the legal requirements of the Law and opened the way into the Holy of Holies through His Blood; He became our mercy seat. In Him, we are now called to become the mercy seat for the world. The mercy seat is the place of forgiveness and restoration. It's the place where the goodness of our Father is released to and through us. Healing flows out of the presence of God to the broken world. **John 20:21–23 (NKJV)** is a beautiful example of us now being the mercy-givers to the world; **"So Jesus said to them again, peace to you! As the Father has sent Me, I also send you.' And when He had said this, He breathed on *them* and said to them, 'Receive the Holy Spirit. If you forgive the sins of any, they are forgiven them; if you retain the sins of any, they are retained.'"**

John 14:12 (NKJV) is a promise for all who live in the Presence of the Father. This portion follows the words of Jesus, saying that He would prepare a place for us with the Father (the Most Holy Place). This is one of the most prominent promises of Jesus and needs to be interpreted in the context of the previous text: **"Most assuredly, I say to you, he who believes in Me, the works that I do he will do also; and greater works than these he will do, because I go to My Father."**

This is a promise for those who understand that they are seated with Jesus at the Father's right hand and know that we now have the same authority that Jesus has. We are God's mercy seat for the world. The Third Room, Most Holy Place, is the primary place from where we minister to the world. This is the place from where we preach, heal, and bring deliverance. Are you there? Are you believing and receiving your inheritance in the Promised Land, the place of the Father?

Let us summarise what the meaning and actions learned from the Third Room, the Most Holy Place, mean to you personally.

- Enter into and live in Father's presence with Spirit-led worship and praying in the Spirit.
- Embrace the fact and privilege of living at the Father's right hand with Jesus.
- You are invited to sit with Jesus and rule over this world and creation.
- You are invited to come and fellowship with Father in a place of intimacy.
- Receive the miracle that the Church of Jesus, and you, as an individual, are becoming the Mercy Seat. The three articles inside the box are your life's principles: Give grace and share the goodness of the Father; love God and your neighbours unconditionally and align and submit yourself to Godly anointed leaders and become accountable to them.
- Be the Mercy seat of God by forgiving people, healing the sick, bringing freedom to the captives, and preaching the Good News.
  Praying with the authority of Jesus (in His Name), declaring the plans and will of the Father.

The Church of Jesus Christ is called to live from the Third Room in this season of restoration and Reformation!

After the Philistines returned the Ark of the Covenant, King David placed it on Mount Zion in Jerusalem and created a free worship experience for all around the Presence of God. In the same manner, we are destined to bring every believer into the presence of God through the Blood of the Lamb.

God (tangibly present in our midst) is the focal point of our worship, and no one and nothing else may be allowed to be central in our service to God. The Sacramental Churches focus on the sacraments of communion and baptism to be central; the Reformed Churches focus on the Bible to be central, and the Baptist Churches centre around the activity of baptism. Many things have become the centre of worship; it could be the preacher, the musicians, the people, or the building. Yet, too rarely is the presence of God (Ark of the Covenant) celebrated as the central focus of corporate worship. The people of God, Israel, with Moses in the desert, did not meet to hear or deliver sermons as most Churches do today, but their celebration was focused on the manifest presence of God (cloud and pillar of fire) in their midst. God spoke out of the manifestation of His glorious presence.

Christ's Third Reformation is about Him utilising His own Church to fulfil God's original mandate to humanity, to subdue all things, take dominion, and fill the earth. This is the season of the Most Holy Place, the Third Room, the Place of the Father! This is the season the Church is moving into; The Altar of Incense burning at the entrance of the Most Holy Place, the Church becoming a generation of worshippers, worshipping the Father in Spirit and Truth. A Church seated with Christ at the Mercy seat, at the Father's right hand. A Church doing the same works as Jesus did and even greater works. A Church operating in the presence of God, releasing the Glory of God to cover the whole earth and discipling nations and every ethnic group. This Church is being restored to the original meaning of the Ark of the Covenant. A Church operating with Angels, offering God's mercy and goodness, carrying the grace of the manna, the principles of love of the stone tablets and the staff of Aaron, divinely aligned with God's leadership.

This Third Reformation will bring about a change in thinking regarding the goal and purpose of the Church. Most Evangelical and Pentecostal theologians see no other purpose for the Church than to 'win more souls to Christ in preparation for

Heaven. Now we are receiving revolutionary, reformed thinking from the heart and mind of God. The expanded goal and vision of the Third Reformation Church are to co-labour with Christ in His passionate desire for the fulfilment of the promise that "His glory will cover the earth" and also **Revelation 11:15 NKJV: " ...there were loud voices in Heaven, saying, 'The kingdoms of this world have become the Kingdoms of our Lord and of His Christ, and He shall reign forever and ever!'"**. It is all about rulership and establishing the Kingdom of God, manifesting through Jesus Christ, to whom all authority in Heaven and Earth was given.

Daniel's interpretation of Nebuchadnezzar's dream of a great statue being demolished by a small rock is a prophecy from the Old Testament, which is now being fulfilled in our age. In this coming Kingdom, which is *now,* God's people are being raised to full godly stature! That rock is becoming powerful and will eventually cover the whole earth! This is the coming Kingdom of God, the rock is Jesus Christ, and that is the Church's mission. **Daniel 2:44 (NKJV) "And in the days of these kings the God of heaven will set up a Kingdom which shall never be destroyed, and the Kingdom shall not be left to other people; it shall break in pieces and consume all these kingdoms, and it shall stand forever.."**

Signs of this season or this Reformation started to surface worldwide over the last fifteen to twenty years and include:

- A focus on God's presence as the primary activity of meetings and activities within the Church.
- Intense, passionate, and intimate worship become the primary focus of the Third Room reformation.
- Intercession and spiritual warfare are done within the courts of Heaven, the Most Holy Place.

- The awareness of angels serving and ministering to and with the sons of God.
- The 'mercy seat' ministry of grace, healing and forgiveness are becoming central and prominent.
- The principles of righteous living according to the given Law in the time of Moses are restored in the abundant love of the Father. Sons of God learn how to operate with the Law of abundant love written on their hearts.
- They are aligned with, connected and accountable to apostolic leadership and spiritual fathers - a worldwide Church phenomenon.
- Acknowledging authentic apostles and prophets is becoming a reality in this third Reformed movement. For this reason, some call it an Apostolic Reformation.
- What the First Reformation declared as a newfound Biblical principle is now daily practice, and that is what the priesthood of all believers is all about. Every son and daughter of God is now called a full-time minister with Jesus. Everyone can minister, testify, heal, deliver, pray and read and interpret their Bible. Everyone can access the Father and hear the Father's voice themselves.
- The Church of Jesus is restored to real family life, and the performance ministry of orphans is replaced with powerful resurrection life. We are living naturally supernatural! The Kingdom of God is family. The triune character of God as Father, Son and Holy Spirit reflects real family intimacy.

Especially in the Third Room (the Third Reformation), the promises of God are becoming a reality for the sons of God:

- **Dominion to rule and to overcome.**
- **Representing and revealing the Father – the Father's heart.**

- **Intimacy with the Father through Holy Spirit-led worship.**
- **The voice of the Father becomes evident to the sons.**
- **Supernatural wisdom becomes the privilege of the sons.**
- **Miracles, signs, and wonders are part of the grace of the mercy seat.**
- **Kingdom wealth creation is a reality, and it is the inheritance of the sons.**
- **Supernatural unity in relationships, marriage & families become a given lifestyle.**

14. PAUL, OUR EXAMPLE OF SPIRITUAL FATHERHOOD

1 Corinthians 4:15–17 (NKJV) "For though you might have ten thousand instructors in Christ, yet *you do* not *have* many fathers; for in Christ Jesus I have begotten you through the gospel. Therefore I urge you imitate me. For this reason, I have sent Timothy to you, who is my beloved and faithful son in the Lord, who will remind you of my ways in Christ, as I teach everywhere in every Church."

Spiritual Sons of Paul

We will look at some of the best examples of the sons of Paul, three prominent men who were called sons of Paul:

Timothy

Timothy was found by Paul, a young man who would become his **"dearly beloved son" (2 Timothy 1:2 (NKJV))**.

Timothy had no father! His mother and grandmother raised him. Paul trained and fathered him. Paul reminded him: Don't forget your prophetic Word!

Finally, we see someone like Paul imparting to Timothy as a Son, resembling many of these Principles:

- Timothy is called a son by Paul
- Timothy served Paul (Ministered)
- Timothy was Paul's student disciple
- Paul sent Timothy
- Timothy was commanded to imitate Paul
- Timothy was to take the words (pattern of sound doctrine) of Paul and give them to faithful men

A son in the ministry must place his life into the hands of a spiritual father. This vulnerability is an openness to change and impartation (most people build a wall around them because of their past hurts – but now is a new season). It is a quality of trust that a child has for his father!

If Timothy was to minister the gospel effectively, he had to yield his life to Paul. The son must fully trust his father to perform painful surgery in proper righteousness.

1 Timothy 1:2 (NKJV) "To Timothy, a <u>true son</u> in the faith: Grace, mercy, *and* peace from God our Father and Jesus Christ our Lord."

2 Timothy 1:2 (NKJV) "To Timothy, <u>a beloved son</u>:

Grace, mercy, *and* peace from God the Father and Christ Jesus our Lord."

Philippians 2:19–30 (NKJV) "But I trust in the Lord Jesus to send Timothy to you shortly, that I also may be encouraged when I know your state, for I have no one <u>like-minded</u> who will sincerely care for your state. For all seek their own, not the things which are of Christ Jesus.

But you know his proven character, that as <u>a son with *his* father, he served with me in the gospel</u>.

Timothy was a true and faithful son. Paul calls him; a beloved son and like-minded son. Timothy surrendered his life to his spiritual father. His father trained and released him to do the same ministry as Paul. He served and obeyed his father even to a place of pain (Paul expected him to be circumcised).

Titus

Titus 1:4 (NKJV) "To Titus, a true son in *our* common faith: Grace, mercy, *and* peace from God the Father and the Lord Jesus Christ our Savior."

Titus was of gentile heritage and remained uncircumcised, as seen in Galatians 2:1-3. This passage shows Titus accompanied Paul to Jerusalem, and other passages show he assisted Paul on some of his journeys (2 Corinthians 7:6–7; 8:6, 16).

The letter to Titus shows the concerns both men had for the challenges the members of the Church of God faced. They shared a trusted relationship based on their calling and belief in God and Titus' desire to do things honourable and godly.

Onesimus

Philemon 1:10–11 (NKJV) "I appeal to you for <u>my son Onesimus</u>, whom I have begotten (became his father) *while* in my chains, who once was unprofitable (worthless) to you, but now is profitable to you and to me."

Though the length of Paul and Onesimus's stay together is unclear, Paul's letter clarifies that Paul has grown very fond of Onesimus.

On behalf of Onesimus, Paul, still imprisoned in Rome, wrote his letter to Onesimus's master, Philemon. The apostle pleaded with Philemon to accept Onesimus back, not as a slave but as a believer and a brother in Christ. Paul cared deeply for Onesimus because the young man had greatly blessed him. Onesimus had been so helpful that Paul longed for him to stay at his side: **Philemon 1:12–14 (NKJV). "I am sending him back. You, therefore, receive him, that is, my own heart, whom I wished to keep with me, that on your behalf he might minister to me in my chains for the gospel. But without your consent, I wanted to do nothing, that your good deed might not be by compulsion, as it were, but voluntary."**

Barnabas (Paul became a son to him)

In the Book of Acts, we find a Levite from Cyprus named Joses (Acts 4:36), whom the apostles called Barnabas. That nickname translated as "Son of Encouragement" (Acts 4:36–37) or "Son of Exhortation" was probably given to him because of his inclination to serve others (Acts 4:36–37, 9:27) and his willingness to do whatever Church leaders needed (Acts 11:25–30).

He is called a "good man, full of the Holy Spirit and faith." Through his ministry, "a great number of people were brought to the Lord" (Acts 11:24). The Bible uses Barnabas as an example of one with a proper perspective on money and property. He brought the proceeds to the apostles when he sold his land and laid it at their feet (Acts 4:36–37).

Despite Herod's persecution, Barnabas was called by the Holy Spirit to go with Paul on a missionary journey as the early Church began to grow. Barnabas' cousin, John Mark, served him and Paul as their assistant (Acts 13:5).

During that first mission trip, for an unspecified reason, John Mark left them and did not complete the journey (Acts 13:13). However, Barnabas continued with Paul. He was with him when Paul's ministry was redirected to reaching the Gentiles with the Gospel (Acts 13:42–52).

After that first trip, Paul and Barnabas began planning their next journey. Barnabas wanted to take his cousin, but Paul refused, and a rift grew between them to the point that they parted company (Acts 15:36–41).

True to his nickname, Barnabas took John Mark and spent time discipling him. That ministry was so effective that, years later, Paul specifically asked for John Mark to come to him, as Mark had matured to become helpful to Paul in his ministry (2 Timothy 4:11).

An unknown person once released a prophetic word: "I raised up Barnabas for one reason: to promote Paul. There are so few Pauls today because so few want to be a Barnabas. I must have a Barnabas before I can release a Paul." I sensed the Holy Spirit saying, "The Spirit of Barnabas will be unleashed in the Church."

Many people overlook Barnabas's important role in the early Church. It is so amazing that Barnabas found Paul and then took him to the apostles in Jerusalem. The apostles didn't think Paul would fit in. They were unsure if he was sincere or even saved.

Following are a few scriptures explaining to us the kind of relationship Paul and Barnabas had:

Acts 9:27 (NKJV) " **But Barnabas took him** (went and found him) **and brought him to the apostles. And he declared to them how he had seen the Lord on the road, and that He had spoken to him, and how he had preached boldly at Damascus in the name of Jesus.**"

Acts 4:36–37 (NKJV) "And Joses, who was also named Barnabas by the apostles (which is translated Son of Encouragement), a Levite of the country of Cyprus, having land, sold it, and brought the money and laid it at the apostles' feet."

Acts 9:26–27 (NKJV) " And when Saul had come to Jerusalem, he tried to join the disciples; but they were all afraid of him, and did not believe that he was a disciple. But Barnabas took him and brought him to the apostles."

Acts 11:22–26 (NKJV) "Then news of these things came to the ears of the Church in Jerusalem, and they sent out Barnabas to go as far as Antioch. When he came and had seen the grace of God, he was glad and encouraged them all that with purpose of heart, they should continue with the Lord. For he was a good man, full of the Holy Spirit and of faith. And a great many people were added to the Lord. Then Barnabas departed for Tarsus to seek Saul. And when he had found him, he brought him to Antioch. So it was that for a whole year, they assembled with the Church and taught a great many people. And the disciples were first called Christians in Antioch."

Acts 13:1–2 (NKJV) " Now in the Church that was at Antioch there were certain prophets and teachers:

Barnabas, Simeon who was called Niger, Lucius of Cyrene, Manaen who had been brought up with Herod the tetrarch, and Saul. As they ministered to the Lord and fasted, the Holy Spirit said, "Now separate to Me Barnabas and Saul for the work to which I have called them."

Acts 15:36–41 (NKJV) "Then after some days Paul said to Barnabas, "Let us now go back and visit our brethren in every city where we have preached the word of the Lord, *and see* how they are doing." Now Barnabas was determined to take with them John called Mark. But Paul insisted that they should not take with them the one who had departed from them in Pamphylia and had not gone with them to the work. Then, the contention became so sharp that they parted from one another. And so Barnabas took Mark and sailed to Cyprus; but Paul chose Silas and departed, being commended by the brethren to the grace of God. And he went through Syria and Cilicia, strengthening the churches."

Apostolic fathers have grace and anointing to impart courage, affirm identity, and release blessings into their sons and daughters, empowering them to succeed and fulfil their destiny.

15. A SON OF A SPIRITUAL FATHER

Father-Son Dynamics

Isaiah 9:6 (NKJV) "For unto us a Child is born, unto us a Son is given; and the government will be upon His shoulder. And His name will be called Wonderful, Counselor, Mighty God, Everlasting Father, Prince of Peace."

The principle is that children are born, but only sons are given. Not everyone that is born in the Church is a son to a father in ministry. The principle is that to as many as believed him, they become sons (John 1:12). When we believe God, we become His sons. In ministry, there are people that get saved in Church, but they are not sons of the house yet. They are not sons; they are just people that are believers. They are just people in the Church. However, when individuals develop and become sons, they become part of God's government. Children are born. Sons are given. The government is on the shoulders of the sons, who become the formulators of government.

"And his name shall be called ..."
That is the DNA. Once people can handle government, the house's DNA is legally transmitted to them. People do not have the DNA of the house because they are not willing to have governmental structures in their lives. They are unwilling because they have not been given as sons. They are just children born. Governmental structures are the house rules.

Again, children are born. Sons are given. The government is established, and DNA is determined. Once that DNA is determined, then you can start naming these kids.

"And His name shall be called Wonderful, Counsellor, the Mighty God, the Everlasting Father, the Prince of Peace" Isaiah 9:6 (NKJV)

Fathers establish government.

This is order, structure, strategy and systems. It is the impartation of life and blessing. The reason many children are never named is that they do not have the DNA of the house. They do not have the established government that the father set in order. Once sons are given, they will look at an order of established spiritual government.

Fathers establish revelation and build an inheritance.

That is wisdom, knowledge and understanding. Also, that is a creative force of spiritual and physical assets. Fathers create mantles that can be passed on for generations. With their life experience, fathers' mantles grow longer every year. Their beards grow longer and longer. Their shadows grow longer and longer. Their influence and measure of rule grow wider and wider, which becomes an inheritance for their sons.

Fathers build intercessors.

These intercessors can push the children through so that the children can be named correctly. When given into an establishment that fathers have built, sons are no different to servants (Galatians 4:7). A son, while a child, is no different to a servant. They are the same, except the son will become mature one day, get the inheritance, and be separated from servants.

Many sons never come into an inheritance because they never serve what the father has built. They never serve that, and they never graduate towards an inheritance. Sons have to understand how they have to serve. Serving does not mean polishing shoes, washing the car, carrying water, a handbag and a briefcase. That is fake.

Sons serve the father's vision.

They commit themselves to the father's vision. They nail their ear to the doorpost with that vision. They learn to interpret the high-level revelation that the father has given. They understand how to take that revelation, work it, and graduate it to the next level.

Sons that are given can be intercessors for their fathers. They can pray the vision, pray for their father, and pray for the oversight so that they are not only covered but also provided a covering. Sons are able to watch a father's back, which is extremely important. Sons are able to open Heaven based on a father's revelation. You look at this in the life of Jesus. Sons can open Heaven. They can do stuff their fathers may not be able to do. Sons have that capacity. That is why you have to have given sons.

A father, as a head and leader, brings direction and correction.

Direction and correction are vital for the success and survival of the 21st-century Church. Direction and correction are not encouragement, necessarily. Sons bring to their fathers as the head, issues and problems that must be addressed and reconfigured for the future. As head and leader, the father provides vision and creates opportunities for provision. Spiritual fathers should be mature and not novices. Fathers produce ways of engagement.

God's heavenly order for earth

Heaven is a representation of family! A perfect triune image of God has been given to human families on earth. We must apply Heaven's ideal union and order to our Church and personal families. The Kingdom of God should be whole, healed and restored families.

God's order and ultimate purpose for His sons and daughters are that sons reveal the Father to this fatherless generation. That principle expects God's sons and daughters to copy Jesus's example as the perfect Son to the Father. The heavenly relationship of sons of God to God the Father should reflect similar behaviour towards our earthly spiritual fathers and even our earthly fathers.

God the Father sent His Son to earth! In the same manner, spiritual fathers send their spiritual sons into the world.

God is restoring us to authenticity and integrity in Him, which redefines our understanding of what it means to be the 'Church'.

This restoration process is a new wine of revelation unto the Church, which forces us to revisit and reconsider the structure within which the Church operates.

The new wineskin is called the House of the Father, Household of Faith or a House of Prayer. In this context, God is illuminating the importance of the Godly relationship of Father and Son and Father to sons.

Fathers are those who take up the spiritual burden, responsibility and importance. Moreover, as Abraham in Genesis 18:19 did, fathers should teach and command the sons in his House to keep the way of the Lord and not depart from it. Similarly, like Paul in 1 Cor. 4:15–16, fathers are those who would urge, command and teach their sons to follow their examples in the Lord, travailing for them, as in childbirth, until Christ be formed within them (Gal. 4:19).

Apart from this genuine concern for spiritual sons, one of the primary functions of fathers is to foster accountability, to stimulate righteousness and integrity, and to replicate and transfer the deposit of Christ within themselves.

Sons (disciples – disciplined ones) listen to the commands of their fathers and become the fruit of the father's instructions (Prov. 3:1).

Disarray, disorder, and weak discipline have robbed us of experiencing the fullness of God's life that He desires to manifest through us as a corporate body.

This life will flow only as the Body comes into unity and aligns with God's order; there (in God's order), the Lord commands the blessing (Ps. 133).

This order of God is primarily evidenced by the context of the relationship God the Father has with His Son, Christ Jesus – the perfect Son and prime example.

God sent His Son into the world (John 3:16) with clear instructions for humanity's salvation and restoration.

A father must send sons into ministry; they cannot simply go and do as they see fit. Jesus obeyed His Father's every instruction, doing only His will and not that of His own (John 15:19).

Jesus aligned Himself accurately with His Father and in absolute submission and obedience. He operated from a position where the blessing was commanded (Ps. 133), where He was clothed with the fullness of the anointing, power and favour of God (Col. 2:9), and where He heard the voice of the Father proclaiming over Him: **"This is My beloved Son, in whom I am well pleased. Hear Him!" (Matt. 17:5–6 – NKJV).**

How do I choose a father?

"God sets the solitary in families" Psalm 68:6 (NKJV)

Most of the time, God Himself assigns the spiritual father He chooses for you. As our all-knowing Father, He knows exactly with whom to set us and who can help us mature into His Fatherhood. Of course, this must be a man of God who can lead you into fuller maturity and a relationship with God. When God sent Elijah to Elisha, He had already told Elijah that he should be Elisha's spiritual father: " (1 Kings 19:16)

Here is another essential point for a spiritual son: A true son walks with his father. A son should be with his father through thick and thin, helping pay the price to bring his commission to pass and faithfully standing by him, no matter what others may do. Once one has been formed and made into a faithful son, with no guile or self-agenda, who carries forward the commission God gave to their spiritual father, they may be sent out geographically by that spiritual father to expand the commission. Now, there are always those sons who remain with the father, helping their father bring to pass the original commission. Either way, during the critical formative processes, the son must be with the spiritual father. Jesus called His 12 disciples that they should be with Him. The apostle Paul took Timothy with him, of whom Paul boasted in **Philippians 2:22 (NKJV), "But you know his proven character, that as a son with *his* father he served with me in the gospel."**

You may previously have had other men of God in your life who have imparted to you in ascending levels of moves of God. Still, they may not be your ultimate spiritual father - the one who can lead you into the complete apostolic move of God and full-fledged Fatherhood! God, in reality, has, most of the time, a spiritual father chosen for you. A father who will bring you up into the fullest dimension of Fatherhood.

What spiritual sons should know:

1. How to honour
2. How to serve
3. Obedience
4. The importance of labour
5. To serve their father's dreams
6. How to minister
7. How to give
8. Loyalty
9. How to be accountable Luke 16:1–4, 8
10. How to create and serve a vision
11. Integrity
12. How to pray effectively
13. Teamwork and brotherhood

What applied to Jesus the Son of God also applies to us who are sons of God: Spiritual sons serve their father's vision! Sons, please (make happy) the father! Sons position themselves to receive from their father. Sons honour their fathers. Sons are willing to be sent. Sons carry the family name. Sons cover their father's nakedness (Noah and sons). Sons are to do what their father does (Jesus and Paul said; Imitate me!) Sons honour their parent's memory. Sons create a culture of sonship (a culture of being adopted). Sons know who they are! Like Jesus, who many times declared, I am! Sons are teachable and available. Sons reflect the image of their fathers. Jesus said: If you see Me, you have seen the Father.

Sons can be intercessors for their fathers. They can pray for the vision, their father, and the oversight so that they are covered and provided a covering. Sons can watch a father's back, which is extremely important. Sons can open Heaven based on a father's revelation. They can do stuff their fathers may not be able to do. Sons have that capacity. You look at this in the life of Jesus. That is why you have to have given sons.

Study the qualities of a spiritual son and a genuine spiritual father. The following guidelines may help you on this journey:

1. Discover your identity as a son of God. I am a son of God, my Father.
2. Develop your intimate relationship with ABBA Father. You come to the Father through Jesus Christ. He is the Way, the Truth and the Life. No one can come to the Father except through Him!
3. Listen to Jesus, listen to Father. Focus on the presence of Holy Spirit.
4. Ask God to connect you to a genuine spiritual father. If you don't find one immediately, wait!

Different kinds of spiritual sons

1. Timothy > A like-minded son, beloved son, trustworthy son.
2. Benjamin > Son of my right hand
3. Barnabas > Son of encouragement
4. Joseph > Son of increase and favour
5. Mephibosheth > A lame son to be covered by the father's covering. He was Jonathan's son and was cared for by David.
6. Prodigal son 1 > Unbroken and rebellious son. Give me ...
7. Prodigal son 2 > Broken and servant son. Make me ...
8. Older brother, son of offence > living outside the House of the Father. Demand attention ...
9. Son of double portion > Elijah – Elisha
10. Joseph's sons: Manasseh > God's healing and restoration (to forget). Ephraim > Son of double blessing

David, the anointed, obedient, honourable son, was obedient to his own father, who apparently rejected him. David obeyed and honoured Saul as his new father even unto near death. David found his real spiritual father in Samuel the prophet.

I am taking you on a journey of sonship transformation! Jesus was called by His Father, 'My beloved Son! What kind of son are you?

You are becoming a son of God. You are becoming a beloved son of a father, which God will bring into your life. You are becoming a father of sons!

I pray for you to become a trustworthy son of Father. I release on you the Spirit of sonship and the heart of the Father! I release direction to you to find your family, the family of God. I also pray that Barnabas's (Holy) Spirit will be unleashed into the Church of Jesus.

16. THE DIFFERENT KINDS OF SPIRITUAL FATHERS

Mal 4: 5–6 (NKJ) "Behold, I will send you Elijah the prophet before the coming of the great and dreadful day of the Lord. And he will turn the hearts of the fathers to the children, and the hearts of the children to their fathers, lest I come and strike the earth with a curse."

We are living in the days of Elijah. Essential to this calling is the turning of the hearts of the fathers toward the children and the hearts of the children toward the fathers. The context is a wineskin of intimacy between leadership and disciples. This begs the dismantling of the clergy-laity institutional model of most traditional churches, which does not transmit grace. The 'father-son' model, which is not gender-based, demands intimacy and a sustained lifelong relationship with the spiritual son. This means the father cannot be fired, retrenched, transferred, or retired. Only death separates the relationship.

We begin our chapter with the different types of fathers. In these broader categories, we will grow in our understanding of the relationships that exist with fathering and what expectations there should be for results. Suppose you read this book and have "daddy issues," such as absent fathers, abusive fathers, weak fathers, and so on. In that case, you will experience understanding in more profound and different places than those of us who began with godly, attentive fathers. Do not allow your past to keep you from changing and accepting a better future.

Spiritual Fathers

Regarding the unique topic of spiritual fathering, not all 'fathers' are fathers. Some people have biological sons but are not fathers to them. They have a physical facade of being that, but in reality, they do not father sons. They may only babysit for a while! They take on tasks above their anointing, ability, and actual gifting level. For example, not everyone who pastors a Church is a spiritual father. He may try to father the people in that Church, but he cannot yet fulfil the calling of fathering other people, leaders, and individuals. Therefore, we must understand that pastoring is different from fathering. I remind you of Paul's distinction between mentors, teachers, and fathers in 1 Corinthians 4. When people approach me and ask, "Please, can you father me," they may mean, "Can you mentor me?" Or they may mean can you be my coach, which means the interaction is seasonal and temporary because specific training is needed or requested.

Surrogate Father

Surrogate fathers are sometimes available because of default. When natural and spiritual fathers disqualify themselves through sin and indiscretion, surrogate fathers arise to manage and establish the presence of real spiritual fathers.

In Genesis 39:1–6, Potiphar was a surrogate father to Joseph. Potiphar groomed him and gave him access to a lot of information. Joseph entered manhood because Potiphar trusted him to run his entire household. Jesus also had a surrogate father in Joseph. His Heavenly Father was not with Him physically. His Heavenly Father only shows up when He's thirty years old and says, "This is my beloved Son in whom I am well pleased." Well, where was the Heavenly Father for thirty years? As active as the Heavenly Father was, He was not necessarily visible in Jesus' practical life. The Heavenly Father did not teach Jesus how to read or to count. He didn't teach Him basic manners. That was the responsibility of the surrogate father, Joseph, and his mother. As we see that a surrogate father may replace a physical father, in the same way, we may have a surrogate father in the spirit.

Corporate Fathers

Corporate fathering (the fathers of a city or nation) is the weight of a burden placed on many shoulders in a region. Consider the town where you live. If you have lived there for a while, you start hearing specific names in cycles. These successful, respected, and seasoned voices oversee the city's key areas spiritually and in business, government, and civic participation. Not all fathers in local Church settings may necessarily be fathers in a regional location. The fact that an individual may have a large assembly may not qualify them as a father outside of that large assembly.

Corporate fathers serve as a kind of council, pooling their experiences and understanding to create sound practices for the rest of us to adhere to and follow. This kind of fathering is the anointing of elders that we see in many cities. It is significant for the continuation of the legacy of fathers and leaders in the Church of Jesus Christ.

Women as spiritual fathers:

While more than sixty per cent of Christians worldwide are women and most missionaries are women, we must acknowledge that many women are bold and strong pioneers and leaders. They invade the world and lead many people to Christ, disciple them to maturity. It may also be seen as similar to a single mother raising children. It may not be the best scenario, but God can and will respond with alternative methods to heal brokenness and the dysfunctional world system. The Spirit of the Father can be upon a woman because there are women that God has raised to lead people in and out of different broken life scenarios. The Spirit of Father may come upon that individual because fathering is a Spirit. A woman cannot be a seed carrier, but she can carry the anointing to move in the Spirit of fathering instead of the actual act of fathering. A woman does not have to act like a man to carry the Spirit of the Father.

We have to acknowledge that God is using women in many unique ways and many kinds of ministries. Some of the world's biggest and best Churches are served and led by mostly women.

Deborah

Deborah, as one of the leaders of God's people, called by God, worked with Barak and the leaders, and they effectively fathered the nation in the Spirit of the Father (Judges 4–5).

Naomi and Ruth

This story reads like a New Testament parable with many applications and interesting meanings of words:

Moabite means "no father." They move from the land of no father to Bethlehem, the house of bread. Naomi introduced Ruth to her destiny, to Boaz. A Moabite became part of the royal line, from which King David and Jesus would be born.

The story of Naomi and Ruth is one of the most profound stories, revealing to us the power of fathering (mothering). It is such an example of what should happen between a son and a father (daughter and mother). Let us dive into this incredible story:

Naomi, her husband, and their two sons went to the land of Moab during the famine in Israel. The two sons marry two Moabite girls. After a while, all three men died, and Naomi decided to return to Bethlehem.

Ruth 1:7-8, 14–17, 22 "Therefore, she went out from the place where she was, and her two daughters-in-law with her; and they went on the way to return to the land of Judah." And Naomi said to her two daughters-in-law, "Go, return each to her mother's house." Then they lifted up their voices and wept again, and Orpah kissed her mother-in-law, but Ruth clung to her. And she said, "Look, your sister-in-law has gone back to her people and to her gods; return after your sister-in-law." But Ruth said: "Entreat me not to leave you or to turn back from following after you; For wherever you go, I will go; And wherever you lodge, I will lodge; Your people shall be my people, And your God, my God. "Where you die, I will die, and there will I be buried." So Naomi returned, and Ruth the Moabitess, her

daughter-in-law with her, who returned from the country of Moab. Now they came to Bethlehem at the beginning of barley harvest."

Ruth 2:1–2 "There was a relative of Naomi's husband, a man of great wealth, of the family of Elimelech." His name was Boaz. So, Ruth, the Moabitess, said to Naomi, "Please let me go to the field, and glean heads of grain after him in whose sight I may find favour.'"

Ruth 4:6+14 "So Boaz took Ruth, and she became his wife; and when he went into her, the Lord gave her conception, and she bore a son." Then the women said to Naomi, "Blessed be the Lord, who has not left you this day without a close relative; and may his name be famous in Israel!' And they called his name Obed. He is the father of Jesse, the father of David."

Ruth followed Naomi because of what Naomi did and meant for her. Naomi eventually introduced Ruth to her destiny, her new husband, and Ruth became part of the royal line of King David and Jesus Christ. Naomi acted as a spiritual father (mother) to Ruth. This is what fathers (and mothers) do; give their sons direction and support. They empower their sons to fulfil their destinies.

Double portion anointing from a father to a son: Elijah and Elisha

1 Kings 19:19–21 (NKJV) 'So he departed from there and found Elisha the son of Shaphat, who was ploughing with twelve yokes of oxen before him, and he was with the twelfth. Then Elijah passed by him and threw his mantle on him. And he left the oxen and ran after Elijah and said,

"Please let me kiss my father and my mother, and then I will follow you." And he said to him, "Go back again, for what have I done to you?"'

One of the most significant examples in the Old Testament of someone paying the price for developing a son is the relationship between Elijah and Elisha. Second Kings Chapter 2 sets the stage for a great transition. Elijah knew that he was reaching the end of his life and ministry. As he reflected on this transition, he knew that his mantle would fall on Elisha—for God had told him. One day, Elijah approached Elisha as he was ploughing the field. Without any fanfare, he placed his mantle upon this spiritual son. Elisha did not rely on his mantle only. He did miracles with the mantle of his spiritual father.

2 Kings 2:10–12 (NKJV)" Elisha asked Elijah for a double portion of his spirit. Elijah responded to Elisha, "You have asked a hard thing. Nevertheless, if you see me when I am taken from you, it shall be so for you; but if not, it shall not be so. Then it happened, as they continued on and talked, that suddenly a chariot of fire appeared with horses of fire and separated the two of them, and Elijah went up by a whirlwind into heaven. And Elisha saw it, and he cried out, "My father, my father, the chariot of Israel and its horsemen!" So he saw him no more. And he took hold of his own clothes and tore them into two pieces. And he took the mantle of Elijah that fell from him, and smote the waters, and said, Where is the LORD God of Elijah? And when he also had smitten the waters, they parted hither and thither: and Elisha went over."

The chariot of fire was a distraction that separated the Elijah generation from the Elisha generation. Yet the condition for the double portion of his spirit was rooted in resisting the temptation to focus on the fire and see his father.

Matthew 17:11–13 " Jesus answered and said to them, "Indeed, Elijah is coming first and will restore all things. But I say to you that Elijah has come already, and they did not know him but did to him whatever they wished. Likewise, the Son of Man is also about to suffer at their hands." Then the disciples understood that He spoke to them of John the Baptist."

Elijah is one of the people who have most reflected the Father's heart. Elijah led a life that was an extraordinary example for Elisha. He made a precious investment in the future ministry of Elisha so that he could do even greater things than Elijah ever did. Elijah meticulously mentored Elisha, bringing him alongside so he could know his heart's passion.

God sent Elijah to Elisha. He had already told Elijah that he should be Elisha's spiritual father. **1 Kings 19:16 (NKJV) " …And Elisha, the son of Shaphat of Abel Meholah, you shall anoint as prophet in your place."**

Elisha left his father's house and went to be with Elijah. There were "sons of the prophets" in Elijah's days that were very familiar with Elijah and revered him greatly. However, they did not walk with Elijah as Elisha did. They did not lay down what Elisha laid down to walk with Elijah. They did not pay the price, day and night, that Elisha did. They were not true, full-fledged sons to Elijah. Therefore, they did not receive Elijah's anointing and mantle when he left the earth. They didn't even know what had happened to him! (2 Kings 2:16,17) Only a true son like Elisha will partake of his father's mantle.

The Holy Spirit directs you to accept and receive someone as a spiritual father. Elisha followed Elijah after being called to do so. Real spiritual fathers draw sons to them, not slaves.

For those asking whether we only have one spiritual father in our lifetime? It sounds logical and practical to say yes, but we do not have any Biblical direction to say yes or no. So we will again emphasise the principle that the Holy Spirit must let you and help you!

The following Psalm is a beautiful description of the anointing flowing down from the High Priest to those submitting to him in unity.

Psalm 133 (NKJV)

Behold, how good and how pleasant it is
For brethren to dwell together in unity!
² It is like the precious oil upon the head,
Running down on the beard, the beard of Aaron,
Running down on the edge of his garments.
³ It is like the dew of Hermon, descending upon the
mountains of Zion;
For there, the Lord commanded the blessing— Life
forevermore.

Holy Spirit leads sons to a father.

The Holy Spirit directs you to accept and receive someone as a spiritual father. Elisha followed Elijah after being called to do so. Real spiritual fathers draw sons to them, not slaves.

God chose Eli for Samuel, while Eli was an evil, disobedient father.

David had a weak father, and eventually, as a young man, King Saul became his surrogate father. But Saul wanted to kill him because of jealousy and fear. Finally, David found a father in Samuel, the prophet. Samuel anointed him, prophesied over him, mobilised him into his destiny, and comforted him for many years.

Your biological father may also become your spiritual father. A great example was David to his son Solomon. My own sons have also become my spiritual sons. What a blessing and honour!

In an apostolic culture, relationships are prioritised above doctrinal agreement, promoting highly relational core connections. Apostles create covenantal, family relationships because believers are attached to and through fathers and family, not doctrine. This relational security creates an environment that attracts revelation. This promotes freedom for people to think creatively, dream, envision with God, and experience new depths of the Holy Spirit.

Spiritual fathers are there to establish a spiritual cover and give the sons an accountability platform. Spiritual fathers are there to establish a heavenly government.

Like Elijah to Elisha, spiritual fathers create mantles and make them available through relational connection. They are an excellent example of a double anointing on the son (2 Kings 2:11–12.)

Failed spiritual fathering

The shepherding movement of the 1970s exposed the weaknesses of bad fathers. We observed some problems with the shepherding movement:

1. The father controlled the son, so he was not autonomous in his decisions—overemphasising obedience to the

shepherd. The shepherd made all significant decisions for the disciple.

2. It violated the authority of the shepherd of the local Church in that those shepherds outside the local Church were fathering disciples (sons) that were not their own.
3. Taking oaths, making vows, and signing covenants.
4. Hierarchical "dictatorial" leadership, top-down structure.

Although we have many examples of failed biological fathers in the Bible, we don't have many examples of spiritual fathers who failed. David was fathered by King Saul, who tried many times to kill him. Eli, the High Priest, fathered Samuel. Eli failed horribly with his own children and was no example to Samuel. **1 Sam 2:12 NKJV " Now the sons of Eli *were* corrupt they did not know the Lord".**

As the leading Prophet of Israel, Samuel also failed with his own children. As Samuel ages, he repeats Eli's error and appoints his own sons to succeed him. Like Eli's sons, they become greedy and corrupt (**1 Sam. 8:1–3**).

Eventually, it seems that Samuel fathered and supported King David well.

Good fathering involves the following:

1. The father favours his spiritual son and wants to see his son blessed. The father rejoices when his son surpasses him.
2. The father allows the voice of God to prevail in the relationship. Joseph allowed God to name Jesus and determine his destiny, although he was the earthly father of Jesus.

3. The father resources the son. He transmits grace, anointing, and truth to his spiritual son. This is the Elijah-Elisha transmission.
4. The father is the pacesetter; he pioneers the way for his spiritual sons. His sons then walk the road he has crafted. The next generation's labour is spent building on the foundation laid by the spiritual father.
5. The father demonstrates the Heavenly Father's character.
6. The father governs without manipulation. In the father-son relationship, manipulation and control are not allowed to happen.
7. A true father's heart will not rule you but will serve you and your vision. He will labour to help you fulfil your destiny. True fathers are concerned about the inheritance being transferred to the next generation. They are concerned about preparing that generation to receive all the Father has for them.
8. Giving is the heartbeat of love. The father's heart is revealed on earth when God's heart touches a man's soul and is manifested through that man's life.
9. The ones who begin to emerge as true fathers are men who manifest the same Spirit of Christ, which is the love of God.
10. A father must have a giving heart, but it is not simply about giving things; more importantly, he must give of himself, for that is what the Father in Heaven did. Jesus was Father's love gift to the world. He knew that He could give no greater gift than the gift of Himself.

Real fathers Invest their Life in Another.

The Father gave Himself to humankind in the person of His Son. God visited man in the flesh through His Son, Jesus.

Jesus came to introduce man to the Father's heart and instil the same kind of heart, knowing that man could never accomplish this naturally. We naturally have the heart of a parent and can instruct our children, but imparting His life will require the heart of the Father to be implanted in us. Man cannot do that; only God can do it in us.

A man doesn't become a father because someone has laid hands on him and declared it. A father must be willing to lose his life in Christ to gain the Father's heart. A true spiritual father will be able to envision his son's destiny and, empowered by that vision, will be willing to pour out his life into the life of his spiritual son or daughter. A true father never functions from the place of his position or title. He ministers from a place of spiritual anointing that causes his gift to be made manifest in passionate love.

A father is not a father because someone has said, "You're a father." A man becomes a father when he bears the head of the Father and functions like the Father. According to Paul, a true apostle is not one because of the title but does the work of an apostle. **1 Corinthians 9:2 (NKJV)" If I am not an apostle to others, yet doubtless I am to you." "For you are the seal of my apostleship in the Lord."** For a man to be a true father, the anointing of God must flow through his life in such a way that he brings forth the presence of God in others' lives.

Becoming a father to the fatherless

I pray that fathers who read this book will receive the Spirit of the Father - not just for their own families but also for the Church and our culture. The spirit of a father is the awareness that everyone around him is his responsibility.

Many children have only a biological father, not a true father. Some women and children have lost husbands and fathers to divorce or death. So, as Christian fathers, we must be sure that we take responsibility by praying for these families and supporting them in other ways so that they may be restored to their Heavenly Father's plan for their lives. James wrote, **"Pure and undefiled religion before God and the Father is this: to visit orphans and widows in their trouble *and* to keep oneself unspotted from the world." James 1:27 (NKJV)**

David declared, **"A father of the fatherless, a defender of widows, is God in His holy habitation. God sets the solitary in families; He brings out those who are bound into prosperity, But the rebellious dwell in a dry land." Psalm 68:5–6 (NKJV)**

God's earthly family is His Church!

I believe the Church should form the most magnificent "adoption agency" in this time of the world. You change a nation not by attacking the government but by being a true father to your children and those who are fatherless. That's the way God did it in every situation. Godly fatherhood is the key to this generation and all to come.

God's Son entered this world and had to be adopted by an earthly father, Joseph. Joseph stepped out responsibly and became the earthly father of Jesus, the Savior of the world, at great personal risk and sacrifice to himself.

"On Apostleship & Fatherhood, many who preach the so-called 'Sound' doctrines mostly create separation, denominations, and control! We need authentic spiritual fathers who see the bigger picture (truth) than those with their traditional pet doctrines!" Kris Vallotton

17. THE DIFFERENCE BETWEEN MENTORING AND FATHERING:

God called me twenty years ago to be a father to His people. It took nearly twenty years to mature and understand most of what this calling entails and how it should function.

The secular world is doing a lot to promote mentoring and coaching at all levels of business and operations. But the Church is called to do a complete life transformation programme. Jesus called this programme discipleship.

Jesus said we, as the Church, would do the same works as He, and even greater! The Bible's model of Jesus: "Go! Make disciples …" has been downgraded to a sermon teaching method and a membership enrolment. Very few Churches have a specific disciple-making or training programme that teaches and forms people into radical Jesus followers and demonstrators of the Kingdom of God. This is for all believers! People must be trained, equipped, anointed, and sent out into the world.

Mentoring, coaching, teaching, giving advice, counselling and motivation are short-term actions and a necessary beginning process in mobilising people to be available and ready to start a ministry. But more is required; deeper discipling is needed, which I call fathering in this book.

When Paul addressed the dysfunctional Corinth Church, he said to them, **1 Cor 4:15 (NKJV), "For though you might have ten thousand instructors (mentors) in Christ, yet you do not have many fathers; for in Christ Jesus, I have begotten you (became your father) through the gospel."**

He actually said that the lack of real fathering is part of the problem because they misbehaved and stayed immature. He continued by saying: "Imitate me" as a spiritual father representing the Kingdom of Heaven and our Father of our spirits. Spiritual fathering is much more profound, deeper, and directional than typical mentoring.

Fathering can come from any mature son of God. The father of sons and fathers is typically a mature sage with an apostolic anointing who can father (disciple) spiritual sons and upcoming fathers. Fathering is also a long-term relationship that may even be lifelong.

Mentoring and Coaching

Let's begin by separating the concepts of mentoring and coaching by definition and example. Mentoring describes the interaction between a tutor and a student; there is a reason for the relationship, and students give tutors or mentors room to identify potential in their lives. In Greek mythology, we find the general context of a mentor's role. It is to share knowledge, experience and wisdom with one who has less. The mentor's job was to train, develop, and prepare for the generation of rulership.

Coaching is the directing of potential toward a specific end goal; it is the relationship between an instructor and a receiver where the receiver gains understanding and strategy for success in a defined and developed area.

Mentoring vs Coaching vs Fathering

Fathering is altogether different from mentoring and coaching. A Father goes beyond being a mentor and a coach. A coach can give you keys. A mentor can identify keys, but each may do this without a relationship with you. Once all payments are complete, the mentor and the coach may not necessarily be concerned about your well-being. A coach is with you for a season, but you get another coach because you are going to another level. You may not have a relationship with a coach after finishing their job in a season. But with fathers, the relationship is until death do us part. Thus, you cannot change fathers every time.

A father will invest his life in his son/daughter. A teacher or mentor doesn't have to invest his life in those he is teaching - the teacher and student part when the lesson is done for the day. A teacher doesn't necessarily have to care whether the student understands his teaching. But a father has a personal investment in his sons and daughters and wants to see them do much more than gain knowledge. He wants to see them reach their destiny in God. A man who bears the heart of the Father will, without reservation, give up his life for his children.

God has allowed many of us to be a father to younger people. Man originated from the heart of the Father. The purpose of the Father is to establish that heart in us so that through us, our sons/daughters can be established in Him and arise to more excellent dimensions of spiritual reality.

You need to be fathered! Mentoring alone is not enough!

Fathering begins with, revolves around, and culminates in God the Father. We can be dedicated, consecrated Christians but still not know the Father! There cannot be full fatherhood in any person without that person first coming into and under God's Fatherhood.

Fatherhood goes far beyond a person's training, teaching, counselling, guiding, and what most call "mentoring" another person. But mentoring is not fathering. A mentor is defined as follows: "A wise, loyal advisor or counsellor; a teacher, coach, guide, or tutor." Indeed, these practices are included in and related to fatherhood, but these practices alone do not constitute fatherhood.

A mentor can offer guidance and knowledge, counsel and advice, and even a dimension of wisdom and example. But there are some significant differences between a mentor and a father. A father can be and is the most effective mentor there is. One who is a father is also a mentor. But one who is only a mentor is not a father. The Apostle Paul distinguished between a mentor and a father in **1 Corinthians 4:15 (NKJV)** when he said, **"For though you might have ten thousand instructors in Christ, yet you do not have many fathers; for in Christ Jesus I have begotten you (became your father) through the gospel.."** The word "instructor" in Greek actually means " ...a boy leader whose office is to take the children to school; a tutor ... instructor".

Yes, a mentor or mentoring traits are helpful and beneficial. But a mentor has no authority over your soul (mind, emotions, and will) and cannot produce obedience in you. Only a father can do that! A father gives you his nature and seed. It is inborn - it is the core makeup of your being. Then it is his responsibility to conform your soul to the will of God. So, by his authority, a father will require your obedience to God's truth and will and to all that is right. A true son, like Jesus in the Garden of Gethsemane, will surrender and submit His will and obey the correct will of The Father. A father raises and rears you, forms and moulds you, sets you right, changes and rectifies you. This rightly-wielded, fathering authority that produces and requires obedience to God was found in Abraham. That is why God the Father brought Abraham into his promised destiny to become the father of many nations.

"You do not have many fathers!" This is the cry and prayer in this hour for God to raise mature sons to a level where they can father God's people. The Church structure needs to become flexible to accommodate the heavenly family and be transformed into a godly family.

The wineskin of the Church needs to be renewed and flexible to accommodate the new wine of the godly apostolic function of earthly fathers revealing our Heavenly Father (ABBA).

18. THE ROLE OF THE CHURCH TO FATHER GOD'S CHILDREN

The Church and leaders must do what Jesus and Father God did by sending His Son and sons. Jesus said that those who believe would do the same works as He did and even greater **(John 14:12)**.

Let's imitate Jesus and Father God, even as Paul commanded his spiritual sons: **"Imitate me." 1 Corinthians 11:1** and **1 Corinthians 4:16 (NKJV): "Therefore I urge you to imitate me."**

Philippians 3:17 (NKJV): "Join one another in following my example, brothers, and carefully observe those who walk according to the pattern we set for you."

1 Thessalonians 1:6 (NKJV): "And you became imitators of us and of the Lord when you welcomed the message with the joy of the Holy Spirit, in spite of your great suffering."

Basic principles can be seen in the relationship between the Father and Jesus, Jesus and the disciples, and Paul and his spiritual sons.

Fathers send sons into ministry.

- The Father sent Jesus to the world.

    John 7:28–29 (NKJV): "Then Jesus cried out, as He taught in the temple, saying, "You both know Me, and you know where I am from, and I have not come of Myself, but He who sent Me is true, whom you do not know. But I know Him, for I am from Him, and He sent Me."

- Jesus sent the disciples into the world as the Father sent Jesus, His son.

    Luke 9:2 (NKJV): "He sent them to preach the Kingdom of God and to heal the sick."

    John 20:21 (NKJV): "So Jesus said to them again, "Peace to you! As the Father has sent Me, I also send you."

- A spiritual father in the ministry sends his son into the ministry.

    ACTS 19:22 (NKJV): "So he sent into Macedonia two of them that ministered unto him, Timothy and Erastus; but he himself stayed in Asia for a season."

Fathers confirm sons in the ministry.

- The Father bears witness and confirms the sending of His Son.

    John 5:37 (NKJV): "And the Father Himself, who sent Me, has testified of Me. You have neither heard His voice at any time nor seen His form."

- Jesus bears witness and confirms the disciples.

  Mark 16:20 (NKJV): "And they went out and preached everywhere, the Lord working with them and confirming the word through the accompanying signs. Amen."

- Paul bears witness to Timothy's ministry to congregations where he is sent.

  1 Corinthians 4:17 (NKJV): "For this cause have I sent unto you Timothy, who is my beloved son, and faithful in the Lord, who shall bring you into remembrance of my ways which be in Christ, as I teach everywhere in every Church."

Spiritual sons represent spiritual fathers.

As Jesus revealed the Father, spiritual sons should represent their spiritual fathers. To those to whom He is sent, the Son will manifest the Father in mind, word and deed.

- Jesus did the works of the Father by the power of the Father.

  John 14:10 (NKJV): "Do you not believe that I am in the Father, and the Father in Me? The words that I speak to you I do not speak on My own authority, but the Father who dwells in Me does the works."

- The apostles manifested Jesus to the world.

  The apostles did the works through the impartation of power from Jesus.

  Acts 3:12–16 (NKJV): "So when Peter saw it, he responded to the people: "Men of Israel, why do you

marvel at this? Or why look so intently at us, as though by our own power or godliness we had made this man walk? The God of Abraham, Isaac, and Jacob, the God of our fathers, glorified His Servant Jesus, whom you delivered up and denied in the presence of Pilate, when he was determined to let Him go. But you denied the Holy One and the Just, and asked for a murderer to be granted to you, and killed the Prince of life, whom God raised from the dead, of which we are witnesses. And His name, through faith in His name, has made this man strong, whom you see and know. Yes, the faith which comes through Him has given him this perfect soundness in the presence of you all."

- Timothy manifested his father in the ministry to those Paul sent him to. Timothy has the same mind and will as his father.

Philippians 2:19–22 (NKJV): "But I trust in the Lord Jesus to send Timothy to you shortly, that I also may be encouraged when I know your state. For I have no one like-minded who will sincerely care for your state. For all seek their own, not the things which are of Christ Jesus. But you know his proven character, that as a son with his father, he served with me in the gospel."

- Timothy teaches the ways of his father.

1 Corinthians 4:17 (NKJV): "For this cause have I sent unto you Timothy, who is my beloved son, and faithful in the Lord, who <u>shall bring you into remembrance of my ways</u> which be in Christ, as I teach everywhere in every Church."

- Timothy had an impartation from his spiritual father.

2 Timothy 1:2, 6 (NKJV): "To Timothy, a beloved son:

Grace, mercy, and peace from God the Father and Christ Jesus our Lord. Therefore, I remind you to <u>stir up the gift of God which is in you through the laying on of my hands</u>."

One of the most essential prophetic challenges for the Church is the Malachi 4 mandate.

There's plenty of reflection among Christians about the spirit of Elijah. This Old Testament mouthpiece offers various character traits that his New Testament leaders would do well to model. However, for all the accurate prophetic decrees and miraculous moments that characterised Elijah's ministry, his spiritual fatherhood is perhaps most needed in the Body of Christ.

With companies of young prophets rising and armies of prophetic believers awakening to the order of establishing God's Kingdom throughout all the earth, spiritual guidance is critical to a stable church to which the world will look for answers.

The manifestation of the sons of God depends on spiritual fathers who will invest time and energy in their spiritual children. So as we consider Elijah and his miraculous ministry, let us also consider this mighty prophet's role in shaping the life and ministry of young Elisha, who did far greater things than his spiritual mentor.

You don't have to be an apostle to be a spiritual father or mother. Still, the apostolic reformation is surely ushering in a renewed focus on this relational dynamic that will prepare the Church for its Bridegroom. We are seeing the manifestation of the Malachi mandate that proclaims: **"He shall turn the hearts of the fathers to the children, and the hearts of the children to their fathers." (Malachi 4:6 NKJV)**

I believe thousands of emerging apostles and fathers have gifts within them that are not being released because we don't have fathers that understand the apostolic calling and the need to release them as we should.

One reason for the shortage of spiritual fathers is the lack of a widespread fathering model in former generations. Many of today's local Church leaders were not fathered and did not know how to father others. The apostolic movement is helping to break this vicious cycle with spiritual fathers and mothers and spiritual sons and daughters willing to learn and grow into their respective roles together for the sake of future generations.

I have seen many so-called disciplinary actions by Churches and Church boards and the devastating effect they have had on destroying leaders' lives and their families. I have counselled many families wrongly disciplined by Church boards, where there were no established relationships between them and no grace. The presence of mature fathers was visibly absent.

An independent (rebellious) spirit often causes would-be sons to resist sonship, most notably because of the correction that comes with the relationship. However, fathers who refuse to correct their sons will lose them, as Eli lost his (1 Samuel 2:34; 4:11).

Sonship is not visible in how someone receives encouragement but in how they receive correction. A true son doesn't make his father adjust how he leads; a true son adjusts the course he follows. While ultimate accountability is surely before the Lord, spiritual sonship goes beyond accountability to a willingness to submit yourself to a father who can speak to the blind spots in your life so you can grow.

I think many leaders resist spiritual fathers because they don't want to get permission from anybody to do what they want. It's not about permission-giving. It's about maturity. It's about wisdom. You can enforce compliance, but submission can never be forced.

Another reason some resist the fathering movement is that they have seen and experienced the fake and uneducated leaders in the Body of Christ.

A true father will cut away the flesh - that's what circumcision is - that would encourage the flow of life.

Young warriors are built for exploits, but older men who become spiritual fathers have a burden to impart before they depart. Beyond submitting to the counsel and correction of a spiritual father and receiving the encouragement and strength of that father, true sons honour their father. But honour goes beyond gifts or even submission to include a measure of dependence.

Just as we honour God by asking him to help us with our challenges, spiritual sons honour their spiritual fathers by asking them for insight.

Sometimes we need to be available to the emerging generation as apostolic fathers and help them find the passion, creativity, sense of destiny, and purpose God gave them. Apostolic fathers lay the foundation. Rather than lording a title or office over a spiritual son, they get under them to push them to a higher dimension.

The apostolic movement is a multi-generational movement. Establishing the principles of the Kingdom of Heaven's principles demands spiritual fathers willing to motivate their sons to greater heights. It is up to us as the Church to carry the expression of Christ and represent the Father to a generation deemed fatherless."

The apostolic movement of this season is a fathering movement, restoring not only fathers to their families and spiritual sons to ABBA Father but ultimately restoring spiritual fathers to His (God's) Church! The Kingdom of God is a Family where the King is also our Daddy, ABBA Father!

19. HEALING FATHER WOUNDS AND BROKEN HEARTS

Just because you don't have a father doesn't mean you have missed out. God will work in your life despite this disadvantage. He will place rich deposits of revelation into your own spirit so that you can save the next generation. Many are naturally tempted to ask God, "Why don't I have a father?" The truth is, we still have the same opportunity to go to the next level. Our battles will become the victories of the next generation. If we win, they win! God has promised to be a Father to the fatherless.

Why can't many call God 'Father' or 'ABBA'?

First, most people do not know God personally, even those who call themselves Christians. They never had a significant, life-changing encounter with Father.

Secondly, too many people carry emotional wounds from their childhood relationships with their fathers (and mothers). Emotional trauma is the most significant reason Christians cannot grow and mature and even have dysfunctional identities.

Six Revelations you need concerning life in ABBA Father

1. Discover and identify your own father wounds and the need for deep healing. Ask Holy Spirit to show you your father wounds. Wait on God, worship and ask. Let Holy Spirit reveal pictures, memories, names and traumas related to an abusive or absent father. Remember that a neglecting father is the same as an abusive father. In what way did your father reveal the character of God to you?

2. Understand how to step into sonship from your slave and orphan mindset. Jesus is the way to Father (John 14:6), and Holy Spirit is the one to lead you as a son (Romans 8:14). Remember, you were a slave and orphan before your redemption and transformation. Now your status has changed from orphan to a child of God who may become a son of God.

3. Believe that the only way to the Father's heart is through Jesus Christ.

4. Discover and understand your new identity as a son of God. You become a son of God through birth, to be born again (John 3;3). You are born as a spiritual baby; become a child of God (John 1:12), mature to be a son of God (Galatians 4:1–7).

5. Mature sons are promoted to become powerful spiritual fathers. This is the fulfilment of Jesus' command: "Go therefore and make disciples of all the nations ..." (Mattew 28:19 NKJV)

6. Please take notice of the benefits of being connected to a genuine spiritual father, as I have disgusted in Chapter 16.

How are we healed from broken hearts and father wounds?

1. **You can be healed from the pain in your past caused by your earthly father and those who represented him.**

   Each person must forgive their father or those who acted as substitute fathers. You need to forgive him for not being there when you needed him the most, for rarely demonstrating his love for you, or maybe because he physically, emotionally, or verbally abused you. Maybe your father was never home or died. Forgive and overcome the emptiness and the feeling of abandonment you have as the direct result of not growing up with a father figure. The Holy Spirit is your healer and counsellor! Allow Him to come in and restore and heal all wounds and trauma!

2. **You must establish a close relationship with the Heavenly Father to develop the Father's heart.**

   Approach your Heavenly Father with confidence and call Him Daddy or Father. How can you develop a close relationship with your Heavenly Father? This can be accomplished by believing that you are His son or daughter and that He is your Father. Our Heavenly Father wants the best for His children, and His greatest desire is to have a relationship with each of us, His sons and daughters. Ask and invite the Father to reveal Himself to you. Ask Him to embrace you as a Father to His son or daughter.

   Hebrews 4:16 (NKJV): "Let us, therefore, come boldly to the throne of grace, that we may obtain mercy and find grace to help in time of need."

3. **To develop the heart of the Father, God must give us His heart.**

As we grow in our relationship with our Heavenly Father, God teaches us how to develop our father hearts. He imparts into our spirit His loving heart to transform us into better fathers and role models for our children and our spiritual sons and daughters.

20. HOW SPIRITUAL SONS SHOULD HONOUR THEIR SPIRITUAL FATHERS

To ensure relevancy and practicality within life and ministry, it is essential to have a founded and biblical understanding of this present move of God the Father. God is restoring us back to authenticity and integrity in Him that redefines our understanding of what it means to be 'Church'.

This topic of honour may be one of the most important subjects for the healthy function of the body of Christ. This is more than a topic. It is a Kingdom culture that needs to be developed and matured in a Kingdom lifestyle kind of Church.

Honouring can easily become a fleshly-driven controlling system! I have experienced and been a part of ministries and Churches like that. God allowed me to be among controlling leaders to learn what honouring should not look like.

There comes a point where honour is no longer honour; it's false loyalty!

The Bible has many principles regarding honour, and this chapter's purpose is not to study the detail of it. Please read the excellent books of John Bevere, "Honors Reward", and Danny Silk, "Culture of Honor".

I believe any Church not developing a culture of honour will not grow into a healthy influential ministry that should change the world.

Honour is all about attitude, submission, respect, accepting one another, regard each other highly, loving with no strings attached and how we respond to one another.

Honour is a two-way discipline. As much as real spiritual fathers will honour and empower their sons, sons must honour their fathers correctly.

Correct honouring will build strong
and healthy relationships.

How honour should operate between spiritual fathers and sons.

- **Sons living a righteous lifestyle will seek UNITY and ALIGNMENT with God's heavenly anointing, which should come through Apostolic fathering.**

Unity brings Godly blessings: Following after godly order. Psalm 133 is such a great example, reminding us of the oil (anointing) flowing down from the head of Aaron (the High Priest) down to the bottom of his garment.

Behold, how good and how pleasant it is
For brethren to dwell together in unity!
[2] It is like the precious oil upon the head,
Running down on the beard, the beard of Aaron,
Running down on the edge of his garments.

³ It is like the dew of Hermon, descending upon the mountains of Zion; For there, the Lord commanded the blessing— Life forevermore. Psalm 133 (NKJV)

- **To be obedient to God and your spiritual father.**

Submission does not mean blind obedience! Obedience is, first of all, to God's principles and voice. This is like a marriage relationship. Marriage relationships include mutual submission and, specifically for the wives, submission to their husbands as to the Lord (Ephesians 5:21–22). Submission is a heart attitude which may ask questions and communicate a place of mutual peace and agreement. Your spiritual father's voice should be the same as our Heavenly Father's. Still, he is not perfect yet; therefore, everything should be tested, and confirmation from the Holy Spirit is vital. King Saul's disobedience to the prophet's voice is a great reminder: **"Obedience is better than sacrifice" (1 Samuel 15:22 NKJV).**

- **To be faithful**

1 Corinthians 4:17 (NKJV) "For this cause have I sent unto you Timothy, who is my beloved son, and faithful in the Lord ..."

- **A measure of dependence**

True sons honour their fathers. But honour goes beyond gifts or even submission to include a measure of dependence. Just as we honour God by asking him to help us with our challenges, spiritual sons honour their spiritual fathers by asking them for insight, help and support. Even at times of difficulty, spiritual sons should first talk to their spiritual fathers and be willing to be counselled and even disciplined.

- **Giving**

One of the main ways to honour is offered in the area of our human ability to give. Honour is given by the act of giving, which reveals a son's heart! It gives direction as to how honour should be administered.

Let's look at the Scriptures;

Proverbs 3:9 (NKJV) "Honour the LORD with your substance, and with the first fruits of all your increase".

Finance and substance seem to be synonymous with honour.

2 Chronicles 1:12 (NKJV) "Wisdom and knowledge is granted unto you; and I will give you riches, and wealth, and honour ..."

We find more examples in the Bible of honour through giving: The queen of Sheba gave Solomon loads of gold and other gifts. Wise men from the East brought gifts worth millions to Jesus at His birth. A woman anointed Jesus' feet with costly oil. Barnabas, later to become a leading apostle, laid the money at the feet of apostles during a meeting in Jerusalem. **Acts 4:37 (NKJV) "having land, sold it, and brought the money and laid it at the apostles' feet."**

What was God's order of giving according to the Old Testament? Remember, the Old Testament lays foundational principles for life in the New Testament. The Tithe (a tenth) of the profit became the thanksgiving and the symbolic sacrifice of my everything back to God. The Tithe always goes to the one over or above you, giving you protection and spiritual food.

The people gave to the Levites, the Levites to the Priest, and the Priest to the High Priest.

The first fruit is a second kind of giving, but it might be the most essential act of obedience because it is about your faith in God for your future. In the Old Testament, the first fruit of everyone went to the High Priest.

Tithing was given by everyone whenever there was a harvest or a profit in labour as a sacrifice of thanksgiving. The first fruit was given to the high priest once a year as a prophetic faith seed for the following year's harvest.

No scriptures in the New Testament cancel giving the tithe, the first fruit or the offerings, as a foundational lifestyle principle in the New Testament. We must apply the principle of giving to the New Covenant of the Cross of Jesus Christ. Obviously, the way we practice the principle will look different because we don't have the old style of Levites, Priests and High Priests any more. Jesus motivated the principle of giving in **Luke 6:38 (NKJV): "Give, and it will be given unto you!"** I presume that this applies to all kinds of giving. Ask the Holy Spirit to guide you in correct giving! Never stop giving! Give to obey and give to honour!

- **Sons honour their fathers by being accountable.**

Sons show honour by not holding back part of their hearts for themselves but sharing their dreams, failures and successes with their spiritual fathers.

- **God's order: Fathers send sons**

Sons are not supposed to send themselves into ministry! A great discipline and way of honour are when sons wait and allow their spiritual fathers to send them into ministry. Fathers are defined as those who would take up the spiritual burden and responsibility and who would, as Paul in 1 Cor 4:15–16, would urge, command and teach his sons to follow his example in the Lord, travailing for them, as in childbirth, until Christ be formed within them (Gal 4:19).

Paul, the apostle, is still the best example of sending his sons by laying hands on them, prophecying over them and validating them as faithful, beloved sons.

Acts 6:6 (NKJV) "whom they set before the apostles; and when they had prayed, they laid hands on them."

1 Timothy 4:14 (NKJV) "Do not neglect the gift that is in you, which was given to you by prophecy with the laying on of the hands of the eldership."

Apart from this genuine concern for spiritual sons, a father's primary function is fostering accountability, stimulating righteousness and integrity, and replicating and transferring the deposit of Christ within themselves.

Sons (disciples – disciplined ones) listen to the commands of their fathers and become the fruit of the father's instructions (Prov 13:1). Disarray, disorder and ill-discipline have robbed us from experiencing the fullness of God's life that He so desires to manifest through us, as a Body of Christ.

This order of God is primarily evidenced by the context of the relationship God the Father has with His Son, Christ Jesus –the perfect Son and perfect example. God sent His Son into the world (John 3:16) with clear instructions as to the salvation and restoration of mankind. A father must send sons into ministry. They cannot just go and do as they see fit.

Jesus obeyed His Father's every instruction, doing only His will and not that of His own (John 15:19). Having thus aligned Himself accurately with His Father and waiting in absolute submission and obedience, He operated from a position where the blessing was commanded (Ps 133), where He was clothed with the fullness of the anointing, power and favour of God (Col 2:9), and where He heard the voice of the Father proclaiming over Him: **"This is My beloved Son, in whom I am well pleased. Hear Him!" (Matt 17:5–6 – NKJV).**

MORE ABOUT THE AUTHOR

Sarel van der Merwe and his wife, Thiesa, have been married for 44 years. Sarel has developed and led the Theologos School of Ministry since 1991, training thousands of students in radical Discipleship and Holy Spirit Counselling and Healing. He founded Oasis Christian Church, a family Church in South Africa, which they planted in Kempton Park in 1996. Since 2021, his second son Stefan and his wife, Marlise, have become the senior leaders of Oasis Church.

Dr Sarel van der Merwe and sons

Sarel and Thiesa have three married sons who, with their wives, serve with Sarel and Thiesa in full-time ministry. They have nine grandchildren, who add incredible joy and fulfilment to their lives.

During forty years of full-time ministry, Sarel has become a spiritual father to many sons and daughters. Sarel finished his theological degree and post-degrees in South Africa. In 1999 he obtained his D-Min degree (Doctorate in Ministry) at Fuller Theological Seminary, Pasadena, California, USA. He also completed several Master's programs in Pastoral Healing and Counselling.

Sarel is passionate about establishing the Kingdom of God on earth through prayer, worship and a demonstration of the power and reality of God to all people. He believes that it is entirely possible to establish an authentic New Testament Church in the world today: A Church where believers are affirmed in their new identity in Jesus Christ and their dominion ruling position with Him. A Church where the miracle of character transformation in their lives reflects the image of God, as originally intended at creation. A Church that knows God intimately as ABBA Father.

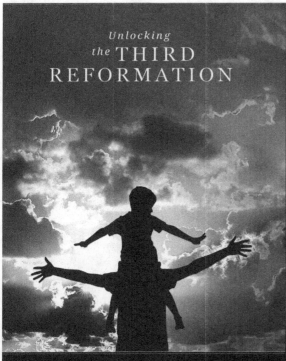

Printed in the United States
by Baker & Taylor Publisher Services